EVERY DAY

⊢ IS ⊢

ELECTION DAY

A Woman's Guide to Winning Any Office,
from the PTA to the White House

REBECCA SIVE

Foreword by Anna Eleanor Roosevelt

CHICAGO
REVIEW
PRESS

*To Steve Tomashefsky, who has been with
me every step of the way. Thank you.*

Copyright © 2013 by The Sive Group, Inc.
All rights reserved
Foreword copyright © 2013 by Anna Eleanor Roosevelt
All rights reserved
First edition
Published by Chicago Review Press, Incorporated
814 North Franklin Street
Chicago, Illinois 60610

ISBN 978-1-61374-662-2

Excerpt ("Ready to Run™ . . . crafting a message.") © Copyright
2012 Center for American Women and Politics, Eagleton Institute
of Politics, Rutgers, The State University of New Jersey, 191 Ryders
Lane, New Brunswick, NJ 08901-8557, (732) 932-9384, fax: (732)
932-6778

For information about special discounts for bulk purchases,
please contact Independent Publishers Group at 1-800-888-4741
or specialmarkets@ipgbook.com.

Cover and interior design: Sarah Olson

Library of Congress Cataloging-in-Publication Data
Are available from the Library of Congress.

Printed in the United States of America
5 4 3 2 1

★ ★ ★

Every day is Election Day. People are
sizing you up every day.

—THE HONORABLE MARY LANDRIEU,
LA, US SENATOR

★ ★ ★

Dear Meagan —
congratulations
on your terrific
work
in sisterhood,
Rebecca

Contents

★ ★ ★

PART III: YOU CAN NEVER CARE TOO MUCH

PART IV: CONFRONT, CO-OPT, CONTROL

Foreword

★ ★ ★

In the spring of 1995, my family joined friends of the Roosevelt Institute to commemorate the fiftieth anniversary of my grandfather's (Franklin Delano Roosevelt, FDR's) death in Warm Springs, Georgia. On that Sunday morning, we gathered in the little chapel there for a service attended by an assortment of dignitaries. Margi, my high school–aged daughter, had been asked to read one of my grandfather's famous speeches—"The Economic Bill of Rights," a portion of his 1944 State of the Union address. Unfortunately, we had missed the rehearsal for the service and were even a bit late. The service had already begun when we were ushered to our seats in the pews. Because Margi had missed the processional, her chair in the chancel with the other speakers was empty.

The order of service proceeded. As the hymn preceding Margi's reading of my grandfather's speech was winding down, Margi rose and started her lonely walk down the center aisle. A seemingly impenetrable wrought iron communion rail stood between her and the other speakers. I could see the slightly terrified looks on people's faces. But, Dr. Forrest Church, the wise presiding minister, reached for the little secret gate just seconds before Margi, determined to play her part, was set to launch a ballet-trained leap over the rail.

Once inside the gate—remember, she had missed the ceremony rehearsal—Margi still didn't know where to go: to the lectern on the left where announcements were made, or to the pulpit on the right where the gospel is read. Being a Roosevelt, she chose the pulpit. From there, she read with conviction an American leader's vision of people, communities, and governments working together to ensure human dignity and opportunity.

Margi played her part that day, summoning her courage and using her gift for public speaking, because she had something politically important to say.

My friend and colleague Rebecca Sive has written *Every Day Is Election Day: A Woman's Guide to Winning Any Office, from the PTA to the White House* to provide guidance for any woman faced with the same opportunity Margi had that day: being a voice in the public square. Now: How do I go about it? The stories Rebecca tells and the lessons she shares from women all over the country have a wealth of wisdom and practical advice about becoming an effective and influential voice and seeking public office.

Margi's great-grandmother, my grandmother Eleanor Roosevelt—ER—was often asked to run for office. A visionary as well as a gifted activist, public speaker, and community organizer, she would have made a great elected official. However, over the course of her public career, she chose other public roles that better reflected what she knew about herself and that enabled her to have the greatest impact imaginable. She joined organizations, headed organizations, hosted gatherings, and took the time to converse with others one-on-one and to help great candidates run for office. All the while, she knew there was possibility around every corner, even as she knew one must take the time to find the right path. *Every Day Is Election Day* will guide you as you take on these roles and pursue your chosen path.

Like other women, ER had many opportunities to turn inward, to narrow her vision and her life's work to a small world around herself. But she taught me—and I have in turn taught my daughters—that our dreams for ourselves are only fulfilled in the context of community. In her book *You Learn by Living: Eleven Keys for a More Fulfilling Life*, ER shares these lessons. One key is "How everyone can take part in politics." Another is "Learning to be a public servant." *Every Day Is Election Day* is a fitting sequel, the ideal guide for every woman determined to find her role in public life in this new century.

No doubt ER—were she with us today—would raise a cheer for each woman who steps up, whether close to home or on the national or global stage. Not only that, but she would be working right beside us, through both victories and defeat, never giving up. Every day, she would encourage us to take her words to heart: be of service; take part in politics and public life; take note; you, too, will feel fulfilled.

—Anna Eleanor Roosevelt
Portland, Maine
December 2012

Introduction

★ ★ ★

For one of my first big evenings out in Springfield, Illinois, as a women's advocate, I went to a cocktail party where I could pay my respects to the African American members of the state legislature. I approached state representative Emil Jones Jr.—who was later to become a state senator, president of the Illinois State Senate, and political guide to Barack Obama—to say hello. As I introduced myself, Representative Jones said he knew why I was in Springfield. I was pushing for a "women's commission" or some such thing. Though the Illinois Commission on the Status of Women already existed, he was right: I was in Springfield pushing a women's cause. Jones said jovially, "Well, I think if there's a women's commission, there should be a men's commission!"

Even he knew that statement was ridiculous. The whole state of Illinois was a men's commission. In fact, the American government is a men's commission. Women occupy fewer than 20 percent of the seats in the US Congress. Only five of our fifty states have women governors. And though thousands of women hold local and state offices, those percentages are dismal as well.

Nevertheless, women's numbers are increasing in the political halls of power. And that's not just good for women. When women who support women's causes win public office, it's good for everyone. They can push government to address women's needs and rights, which affect all of society. They can champion laws that benefit women and their families, which include boys and men. They can make sure women have equal opportunity to lead. Political parity between women and men will be good for America. But we aren't there yet.

Every Day Is Election Day isn't about why we're not there yet. It's also not about why the pace of change is still so slow. It's about changing this sorry state and the role you're going to play in that change.

This book is a practical guide to seeking public office and winning. But your political career won't start there. Nancy Pelosi didn't become Speaker of the US House of Representatives by deciding one day to run for a seat. Deanna Archuleta didn't start out as an adviser to a cabinet secretary. Her first public office was president of the PTA. Archuleta says, "That's where women start from. That spirit of advocacy then continues into elected office."

I'm going to show you how to get started and keep on running. You will learn how every single day is a campaign of one sort or another, and what you need to do to achieve success at every stage.

If you dream of attaining a role of political leadership but fear you're not qualified, or that family responsibilities take you out of the running, or that you don't have the ability to undertake a credible race or raise enough money to win, *Every Day Is Election Day* is going to persuade you otherwise. It's also going to show you that your choice to seek public office will give you cause for celebration. For instance, when Deanna Archuleta became PTA president, her first victory was installing a safe crosswalk for students near a school. She and the other "neighborhood moms" celebrated. When Nancy Pelosi became Speaker of the House of Representatives, her husband of four decades, five children, and eight grandchildren all shared in the joy.

Parts 1 through 4 of this book offer straightforward advice illustrated with the personal and professional stories of women who hold all kinds of offices in many different parts of the country. In the resources section, you'll find information you need to launch your campaign—everything from how to organize it to how to raise the funds you'll need to run (no matter how modest the position you seek or how little money you have) to how to build your visibility everywhere you need to.

My own career in politics informs this book. I grew up outside New York City in the 1950s and 1960s. My father was an activist attorney and politician, and my immigrant mother was a political activist, elected official, writer, and editor. Both of them instilled in me the desire to use my talents to do good for society. Perhaps I'm like you in that way.

I've spent most of my career working with leaders who are women, and I've been one myself. I've campaigned for policies that improve women's status and opportunity, and I've been a public official. I've raised money for candidates and helped them spread the word about their talent for public office. I've advocated for their positions, and I've had a voice in the public square. *Every Day Is Election Day* is for any woman who aspires to have one too.

The women profiled here faced the same challenges you will in winning your elections. Some of them hold elected office. Some hold appointed office. Others run issue advocacy organizations. Others have been political staffers. Still others are nationally and internationally lauded public advocates for women's advancement and equal rights. They are the daughters of Mississippi, as well as Manhattan, but they share some important qualities. They all demonstrate a commitment to public service, and they are unapologetic in their quests for the power to fulfill that commitment. They all sought public leadership as a way to promote policies to benefit women. And they share a joyful and sustaining confidence in their choice of politics as a profession.

None of these women waited for others to grant her permission to excel. None asked others to fight her battles. Each took charge of her own life. Each pursues her political goals every day, beginning the minute she wakes up each morning.

The run-up to Election Day begins much sooner than you might think. Your campaign begins with dreaming big, setting goals, and creating a plan. Completing that plan may take some time, and you will be busy all the while you're executing it. But I guarantee you will experience great happiness along the way. You will also find camaraderie with other women and deep personal satisfaction.

If it's time for your Election Day, and I sure hope it is, *Every Day Is Election Day* is where you should begin. Let's get started.

PART I

EVERY DAY IS ELECTION DAY

Six easy rules

When I first began to imagine writing a guide for women running for office, I went to the bookshelf above my desk for inspiration. I homed in on these titles: *Unbought and Unbossed* by Shirley Chisholm, a Democratic candidate for president in 1972 and the first African American woman to serve in Congress; *Crusade for Justice*, the autobiography of antilynching activist Ida B. Wells; and *My Life*, the autobiography of Golda Meir, the only woman prime minister of Israel and only the third woman ever to hold that position in any country. These memoirs are all by powerful women who were fully engaged in the world, fighting to fulfill their personal dreams.

While I was writing, I kept the following books close by: *Sisterhood Is Powerful* by Robin Morgan, *The Prairie Girl's Guide to Life* by Jennifer Worick, *The Gospel According to Coco Chanel* by Karen Karbo and Chesley McLaren, and *Skinny Bitch* by Rory Freedman and Kim Barnouin. All the authors look straight ahead, without blinders, completely aware of what they need to accomplish. They're all suited up for battle, ready to fight for what's rightfully theirs, which is what Barbara Mikulski, the longest-serving woman in the US Senate, asked of all women after her bill, the Paycheck Fairness Act, failed to pass in 2012. No wishful thinking, no believing that success comes without sweating it out, no illusions about the competition or the discipline that will be required. No matter how inspired they are by the opportunity they seek, they remain clear-eyed and practical.

In *Skinny Bitch*, there's a drawing of a cupcake with devil's horns and tail. The mandate is clear: if you want to be skinny, don't eat cake. While there aren't any line drawings illustrating my key premises, I think they're equally clear.

Here's number one: if you want to be a winner, you have to want it really bad.

My dear friend, neighbor, and longtime mentor Ilana Diamond Rovner, the first woman judge on the United States Court of Appeals for the Seventh Circuit, has a simple answer for how she beat all the politically connected men who'd wanted the same jobs she did. Of course she had to study hard, work harder, and make friends with important people who needed her help. But above all, she says, "It comes down to one word: *desire*."

She goes on: "And I mean raw desire—pure, raw desire."

You gotta want it—bad.

Rule number two is echoed in an article in the October 2012 issue of *Vogue* entitled "The Voice." The article profiles Florida member of the US House of Representatives Debbie Wasserman Schultz, the first woman to be elected chair of the Democratic National Committee. The profile offers a lot of inspiring material: Wasserman Schultz is a breast cancer survivor who kept her illness a secret because, she says, "I just knew there would be well-meaning people who would decide not to ask me to do things because I was going through cancer. I wanted to decide what I was capable of doing." She is a mother of three children who nevertheless pays close attention to others' needs, according to NBC News chief foreign affairs correspondent Andrea Mitchell, who is Wasserman Schultz's friend and also a breast-cancer survivor. But the most telling line is at the article's end, when author Jacob Weisberg says, "It would be foolish to bet against her." That's because of Wasserman Schultz's work ethic: "I might not always convince you that I'm right, and I might not always win the day or be successful on everything I set out to accomplish, but I'm never going to lose because I got outworked." Politicians may rest a little on the seventh day, but they never really quit. That's rule number two. You've got to outwork the competition.

The third rule of *Every Day Is Election Day* is that you will have to win the same way men do. When voters pull the lever or when governors or mayors or school-board presidents make an appointment, they are aware of the candidate's gender. For political reasons of their own or because this woman candidate is making history (as so many do), these voters or officials may even choose to stand with the female candidate on the ticket. That kind of consideration might improve your odds, but it won't be sufficient to win. (Sarah Palin, anyone?) That's because decision makers give the greatest weight to the case you've made. Does your case statement stack up at the top of the pile when it's compared to others'?

Making great speeches isn't a substitute for knowing who your voters are and getting them to turn out on Election Day. Believing in worthy causes isn't a substitute for sensible policy solutions. Learning that "money is the mother's milk of politics" is a prerequisite. There is no "kinder and gentler" way to win in politics that women have and men don't. Campaign tactics are uniform, though the group at which they are targeted differs from one campaign to the next. This is the practical fact.

There are, however, campaign strategies you can deploy that take into account your understanding of women's lives. For instance, being a wife or mother might come into play, as can issues that concern women or the unique alliances you can build among women and with other women leaders because of your shared experience. These realities enable women candidates to create campaign messages or organizing and fund-raising programs that take gender into account in a winning way. Women candidates can do just what, for instance, African American or Hispanic or Jewish candidates do (and Irish and Italian candidates have done even longer): target their community for special understanding and support. And because our life experience differs from men's in fundamental ways that are both biological and cultural, there are ways to win that don't run so much against (female) type that no one will listen to you. You can win with women and for women, and that's my fourth rule.

Rule number five: success in politics is not a one-off. It is a marathon, not a sprint. However, only marathoners willing to switch it up occasionally and sprint when necessary will be successful. Consider an unexpected resignation. Consider the special election because an incumbent has died. You need to be ready for opportunities when they present themselves. Get ready for a marathon career, not a race from a standing start. It won't happen—it never does.

The key to winning an elected or appointed office isn't staking out positions and advocating for them, regardless of the practical realities of getting those positions adopted. That job is for gadflies and true believers. The most effective women leaders are adept at working with other public leaders because they appreciate the constraints of leadership and know how to work within them to achieve beneficial public ends. The art of politics, whether campaigning or governing, is the art of being practical at almost all costs, including making compromises—big ones. If you can't handle that kind of thing, pass this book along to your girlfriend who can.

In the year Jan Schakowsky, a pro-choice member of the US House of Representatives and past Democratic cochair of the Congressional Caucus for Women's Issues, was first elected to Congress, she supported an Illinois gubernatorial candidate who was anti-choice. She asked her supporters to do the same. Most sucked it up and supported him because this particular alliance would enhance Schakowsky's leadership. Though he didn't win, Schakowsky's support did enhance her statewide and subsequent national leadership, including advancing her pro-choice agenda. And she's been a national leader for more than a decade since. Not a bad trade-off. Rule number six: The process of leading and/or governing will be different from the process of advocating.

Consider these your strategic imperatives wherever you find yourself.

Dream big; then set your goals and make a plan

Your dream will inform everything you do to achieve it. You can't win if you don't know what you want. Chances are your dreams don't stop at being vice president. But that doesn't mean achieving second best isn't part of the plan. You'll tell yourself, *I want to be vice president, but only so I can be president one day.*

Your dream and your plan will keep you going on hot summer nights at community meetings, on cold winter days as you trudge door to door, and on rainy afternoons when you're making a speech you've made a hundred times before. The dream will keep you focused on the ideas and the people that matter most to you. That plan will guide you along the path to victory.

I have a photo taken in 1958 showing me at age eight standing pensively in front of my father as he waves to a crowd. I traveled a lot with him during his campaign for Congress, and while I'm sure now that his dream of serving in Congress was what sustained him, I was too young to comprehend much then. However, I'm pretty sure I did understand his practical mission: presenting himself to others and telling them he'd do a good job. My father didn't spring onto the scene as a congressional candidate at the age of thirty-six. Once he identified his dream to serve in Congress, he became active in local politics. He became a steadfast volunteer in town and county campaigns and in the Democratic Party, taking on progressively more responsibility and more leadership roles.

One stop during his congressional campaign was the home base of his opponent, Republican congresswoman Katharine St. George. Tuxedo Park, New York wasn't just any old neighborhood, where you could walk down the sidewalks, knock on doors, and ask to make your case. The wall surrounding it is metaphorical, but the actual entrance was restricted by a guy in a guardhouse. I was eight when I accompanied my father on this campaign stop. I remember the guard telling us, "Nothing doing," when we approached the gate. Was he really saying, "No Jews allowed"? That's what my father told me a few years later, when a swim-team friend invited me to her parents' country home in another private community. My father said, "I'm sorry to tell you this, but you'll never get to go." And I didn't.

Tuxedo Park had been home to the likes of J. P. Morgan and the Astors (and provided the nickname for what had previously been known as a dinner jacket). St. George herself, a first cousin of FDR, had lived there since 1919, and her developer father had built some of its homes. Today, FDR's granddaughter Anna and I are close friends, but in 1958, we couldn't have played together in Tuxedo Park.

Supreme Court justices Ruth Bader Ginsburg and Sonia Sotomayor wouldn't have gotten through that gate, either. Nevertheless, in the face of entrenched cultural biases, they've each dreamed big and made plans for public leadership, too. These two girls shared the goal so many American children of immigrants and ghettos hold dear: *I'm going to make my dreams come true, no matter what impediments I face.*

In 1958, my father's Aunt Flora lived in a second-floor walk-up on 160th Street in New York's Washington Heights neighborhood. One of the joys for my sister and me during our weekly visits with Aunt Flora was playing on the front sidewalk with the Puerto Rican girls who lived nearby. Sonia Sotomayor was a toddler living in the Bronx at the very same time. For all I know, I played with her cousins!

Sotomayor's life offers one remarkable example after another of how she actualized her dream and pursued her plan. Her father died when she was a girl; by her own account, the public housing project the family moved to in the Bronx was run-down and dangerous. Nevertheless, she won a full scholarship to attend Princeton University—this at a time when it had no tenured faculty of Latino origin and few students with a Nuyorican background like hers ("Nuyorican" is a term for a person of Puerto Rican birth who lives in New York City). While she was at Princeton, she led efforts to change university hiring and recruitment practices. After graduating summa cum laude, she went to Yale for law school; then she returned to New York for an appointment as an assistant district attorney and later an appointment to a federal judgeship.

Ruth Bader Ginsburg had grown up in Brooklyn and attended the James Madison High School, just like my father had. In 1959, she graduated from Columbia Law School (also like my father) just a few stops down the subway line from Aunt Flora's. Before transferring to Columbia, Ginsburg had been at Harvard. There, she had a law professor who was so biased against women that he disgustedly told the eight women in her five-hundred-person class that they were taking up seats men should have gotten. Ginsburg didn't let such attitudes get in her way. She says she bore in mind some advice from her mother: "My mother told me to be a lady. And for her, that meant be your own person, be independent." Lesson one on how to realize your goals.

Justices Ginsburg and Sotomayor both had supportive mothers and the sponsorship of powerful men. But neither was afraid to go out on a limb. While you're pursuing your dream, you'll be working alone. A lot. But sticking with it is the only way to get there.

A certain youngster in New Jersey had the idea. She wrote this pledge at the age of ten, already well aware of the destiny she'd be shaping for herself.

What the Preamble to the (U.S.) Constitution Means to Me

"We the people" is the most important part of the Preamble to me. It means I am the government: No king, no dictator, no army will ever take my freedom from me. It also means it is my responsibility to protect my freedoms as outlined in the Constitution. If I am a good citizen, I will accept my role seriously, to be informed and to take part in my government by voting, or, as I hope someday, to be a Member of the House of Representatives.

—*Caroline Casagrande, fifth grade,*
St. Catherine's School, Spring Lake, New Jersey

Caroline Casagrande grew up to take office at thirty-two as a Republican New Jersey state assembly member in 2008. Her district office is in a storefront on Main Street in Freehold, New Jersey (which is also the birthplace of Bruce Springsteen). It's in an old building in an old town, a county seat that's home to the Italian Americans and African Americans who have lived there for decades, as well as to more recent Hispanic arrivals. Her fifth-grade declaration is printed on a poster board that hangs in the office's meeting room.

When Christine Todd Whitman, later governor of New Jersey and director of the federal Environmental Protection Agency, ran for the US Senate in 1990, she sent audiotapes about her candidacy to prospective voters. One arrived at the Casagrande household, where fourteen-year-old Caroline listened to it over and over again. "I listened and realized I could do this," she says. Whitman "showed me what was possible." I'm not sure Casagrande needed Whitman to show her how it was done: in short order, she became president of her grammar school student council, then secretary of the high school student council, and later president of the student government at Penn State.

"Being president of Penn State is no joke," says Casagrande. "It costs a lot to run, and you're in charge of hundreds of thousands of dollars. When I think back on all the power we had . . . We raised our own money. We spent our own money. We had a ton of responsibilities."

Casagrande spent six months in South Africa while that nation rebuilt after apartheid. "People who spoke twelve different languages were working together to build a government. This taught me never to fear anything."

Inspiration, dreams, and a plan notwithstanding, you can't win on Election Day without an army. Whether you're pushing for a big elected office or a high-level appointment, your people are key to your success. At Penn State, Casagrande's campaign staff was a group of college friends, many of whom are now working as political campaign professionals. Though many of them are Democrats, Casagrande says that all of them would "come back and run a big one," if she decided to run for a higher office. Can you say "member of the House of Representatives"?

In 2007, the year Casagrande first ran for the New Jersey state legislature, Governor Jon Corzine "doled out millions," Casagrande says, to local Democrats. She ran anyway, in a majority Democratic district. As a result, she says, "Most people thought [my race] was 'a suicide mission.'"

"I just thought it was what I should do," she says. "I really thought I would be a great assemblywoman."

But that race was part of Casagrande's plan, so she ran. And she won, becoming the youngest woman ever elected to the New Jersey Assembly.

In addition to performing her legislative duties, Casagrande periodically helps run a leadership institute for high school girls in Monmouth County, in hopes of inspiring others by her example. Several of her legislative office interns are graduates. "I do it so they can see a lot of women in positions of power and know that they can change their lives and the world. I've been given this gift of being the youngest woman in the New Jersey legislature, so I want to give them a gift: they can be even younger."

Dr. Gwendolyn Page, superintendent of schools in Mississippi's East Jasper School District, makes an addition to the idea of having a plan: "You've got to ask for what you want and expect to get it."

By way of illustration, Page, who spent her childhood in a three-room shack with no indoor plumbing, remembers a bus ride she took one day a few years ago. As the bus passed the cotton plantation where her grandmother had worked, she realized she was riding next to a fellow teacher whose family had owned the plantation. "I'm thirty-eight now," says Page, "and I have washed clothes on a scrub board. We've come a long way, do you hear me?" Page's mother had said to her, "Why be a nurse when you can be the doctor?" Page took those words to heart, because she never doubted her own ability to get and do the job she wanted. Deanna Archuleta, consultant and former senior adviser to President Obama's former secretary of the interior Ken Salazar, says her mother taught her, "No one is any different from you. No one should be intimidating to you."

In my home state of Illinois, state representative Barbara Flynn Currie is the only woman to have become majority leader of the state House of Representatives. Her suggestion for making a plan to seek a leadership position is to set a goal to become deeply knowledgeable about the issues leadership addresses. Currie took her own advice and became a "policy wonk." By the time she ran for the position of majority leader, her knowledge was greatly valued by her fellow legislators. Currie recounts what happened after she won: "Republican women gave me flowers. Secretaries and staff in the Capitol were thrilled. One of my girlfriends nearly ran her car off the road. The depth of excitement was really quite thrilling."

Molly Bordonaro, former US ambassador to Malta, the youngest woman ambassador in US history and one of the youngest women to ever run for a seat in the US House of Representatives, encourages women to dream big, too. "When my grandmother was my age, she couldn't vote. When my mother was my age, it was unheard of for women to run for Congress. How could I not plan this big given the rights women now have?"

As ambassador to Malta, Bordonaro worked with the US secretary of state Condoleezza Rice, another example of a woman who dreamed big, set goals, and made a plan to achieve them. Bordonaro says she and Rice "connected when I went through ambassador training," shortly after Rice was appointed secretary of state. "She was very specific about what she wanted to accomplish. She wanted to do things very differently. She wanted our national diplomacy to be listening to the people of the different countries, not just to the diplomats"—just as she had insisted the people of our country listen to her.

Bordonaro says Rice "was very good at pointing to the struggles of our own country over slavery and civil rights: this is what we believe in—democracy—but we don't always get it right." Bordonaro goes on: "It was incredibly symbolically meaningful to the message we were trying to communicate regarding democracy, and to what women can be in a democracy. She was extremely effective as a secretary of state because of who she was. The authenticity of our approach was clear."

Ginsburg, Sotomayor, Casagrande, Page, Rice, Bordonaro—all these women dared not only to dream big but to seek successes that subverted norms and societal expectations. Then they made plans to win.

Strategic imperatives for once you've identified the dream and set your goals:

★ Characterize your dream in language that inspires you.

★ "Be authentic about who you are and what you believe," says Cecile Richards, president of Planned Parenthood Federation of America. Use that language to develop goals that are clear and easily explained to others.

★ In your planning, think about the downsides, as well as the upsides, of your choices. For instance, holding legislative office and establishing a history of positions on various issues can actually hinder your ability to win an executive office. Or, if you gain an appointed office and hold it for a long time, it can be hard to make the case that you would be a good candidate for elected office because you have never demonstrated that you can be an effective and empathetic campaigner (the only kind that wins) or of successfully governing while responding to constituent pressure and the exigencies of constantly campaigning. Or, if you've been a staffer, even a senior staffer, it can be hard to make the transition to candidate.

★ Never doubt your right to have the dream in the first place.

Your personality self-test

Certain personality traits are required to achieve success on Election Day. Other qualities can be a bonus. These traits will assist you as you navigate the processes that are inevitable in any campaign. Ideally you'll enjoy those processes. Alternatively, you'll have the intellectual and intestinal fortitude to put up with them.

This self-test will help you to gauge how prepared you'll be for your campaign and how much you'll have to learn to stomach. It will also help you understand which of your stronger qualities will compensate for your weaker ones. For instance, if you're someone who quickly assimilates information and effortlessly processes and makes important decisions but possesses only workmanlike speaking skills, you can make that combination work. Your supporters and your constituents, not to mention sister decision makers, will appreciate your ability and confidence in making tough calls. If you're a compelling fund-raiser in one-on-one meetings with people you know, but you dislike making begging phone calls to strangers, you'll probably be OK, as long as you're willing to make *some* of those calls to strangers.

Consider former secretary of state Hillary Rodham Clinton and her husband, former president Bill Clinton, two highly successful public leaders. Both are smart and hardworking. But he's empathetic while she's determined. He gives long and thoughtful policy speeches that prove his intellectual heft. She downs a beer while dancing in a bar to show she's got a soft side. You too will build and balance your talents and skills as you learn what they are.

Are you a happy person? Though Abraham Lincoln, one of our greatest presidents, was a depressive, I think he's the exception that proves the rule when it comes to public leadership. Most of our leaders exude optimism. They know they need to remain positive, especially in tough times, when people need them the most.

Are you empathetic? The question here isn't whether you like to hug strangers and kiss babies. It is whether you can make a personal connection to other people and care about their experiences. Can you demonstrate empathy in ways that a stranger can feel? For instance, are you willing to be a regular volunteer at your city's homeless shelter or food pantry?

Can you hang with the locals? Can you grip and grin while eating corndogs or chugging a beer? If you can't, it's time to practice. And remember that "down home" doesn't look the same in every neighborhood. But there will always be a way to prove yourself as willing to be one of the locals as well as to work for them.

Can you handle being in the public eye, even in private situations? Monica W. Banks, chancery clerk of Oktibbeha County, Mississippi, told me that her lunch is always interrupted, but she doesn't mind. Her phone is listed. "People call late at night, and I answer." Member of the US House of Representatives Cheri Bustos told me that when she was a candidate for Congress in 2012, her opponent always had a "tracker" at her events, a videographer who recorded every move she made.

Will your family members and friends stick with you through thick and thin? The United States may finally have moved beyond the days when the wife of a male public figure had to stand by her cheating man. But if you get into trouble, you will want your husband, wife, or partner to stand by you. You will want to discuss this scenario, however unlikely, with that partner and other family members. Just in case. And it can't hurt to preview potential minefields with your friends as well.

Speaking of family, do you know your family history? When US senator Elizabeth Warren faltered during her 2012 US Senate campaign over charges she'd mischaracterized her ethnic heritage in order to take advantage of minority status in professional settings, she told the media and the public that she had only claimed what her mother had told her was theirs: a Native American family heritage. Make sure you verify family stories.

And on the subject of fact versus fiction, have you done "opposition research" on yourself? Do you know who you are in public records, in the memories of exes, and in whispered conversations between neighbors or among coworkers? Don't leave anyone out, including and especially those who don't care for you. One of the political movies I recommend you watch is *Primary Colors*, based on the life and lore of Bill Clinton. There comes a point in the story when the candidate for president and his long-suffering wife realize he can't win unless his staff know everything about him. They have to be ready for negative spin about their candidate's alleged infidelity.

Former Democratic congressional candidate Krystal Ball, now an MSNBC political commentator, was derailed during her 2010 congressional campaign when racy pictures of her were posted on two conservative blogs. *New York* magazine described the photos: they "showed Ball wearing a Santa hat with a black bustier. . . . In her hands were a festive Solo cup and a leash attached to a young man, who wore antlers on his head and a Rudolph-red dildo on his nose." Ball lost that race. But two years later she won her next "campaign"—to cohost an MSNBC political affairs show—because she possesses two winning traits: she had the strength to persevere in the face of embarrassment, and she was willing, as she said to *New York* magazine, to "just get it all out there. You have to be totally, uncomfortably honest."

How good are your negotiating skills? My favorite story about negotiating has to do with Eleanor Roosevelt's response to a request from a friend. In 1960, when John F. Kennedy was running for president, he sought the former First Lady's endorsement. She offered it on the condition that, if elected, he would appoint women to high-level positions in his government. After his election, President Kennedy appointed Roosevelt herself, an internationally revered figure, to head the nation's first-ever federal Commission on the Status of Women.

Like Eleanor Roosevelt, you will use negotiation to create change that will benefit others. Unlike Roosevelt, you will also use negotiation to benefit yourself. You may even need to negotiate your way out of a jam to win.

Are you patient? Creating laws and policies, whether as an appointed or elected executive, as a member of a board, or as a legislator, requires constancy with the opposition. Making the sausage takes time. As Barbara Flynn Currie says, "If you're out to change the world the day after tomorrow, this job isn't for you."

Currie told me it took years for her to pass an early-childhood-education bill and then years more to get an appropriation to fund the programs the bill mandated. She liked the process and still does, more than thirty years after her first election. I'd probably shoot myself before it ended. That doesn't mean we both can't (and don't) have roles in the public square. It does underscore the importance of seeking the right public role, based in part on how much you like to negotiate.

Do you have a habit of saying you're sorry? Apologies sometimes have a way of backfiring, by suggesting that the power to have avoided the problem in the first place lay only with you. Because that's rarely the case, work on alternative language for patching up relationships. For instance, practice language about trying harder next time or asking more for advice.

Do you suffer from "imposter syndrome"? In the class I taught on women in public leadership at the Harris School of Public Policy Studies at the University of Chicago, a student asked Currie, a guest speaker, whether she thought "imposter syndrome"—that common affliction where people who achieve success are haunted by the sense they don't deserve it and that they can be found out anytime—is prevalent among women public officials. Currie quickly and firmly said no.

She says those she knows all have healthy egos. Self-doubt can crush a leader, particularly in a fast-paced environment that requires decision making of the "gut check" sort. Gut check yourself on this one.

Can you bite your tongue even when your opponent is clearly in the wrong? Sometimes, you will rebut forcefully. But at other times you will need to remember what your mother told you: "If you can't say anything nice, don't say anything at all." This advice comes in handy when your opponent is about to shoot herself in the foot. Let her do the shooting instead of calling her out for being wrong.

Are you confident? You must have some faith in yourself to even conceive of running for office. But are you confident about your qualifications? In your positions? If your resumé is short ("What do you know?" "You've had no experience"), you'll need to be able to self-assuredly present all your positive attributes.

How green are you? Have you worked up a case for why your youth shouldn't be an issue? Have your closest confidants told you your case passes the smell test? The younger you are when you get started, the further you can likely travel, so this is far from an admonishment to wait. Just be prepared for the naysayers and have your answers at the ready.

Are you willing to pay, and keep paying, your dues? If you think you've already paid all the dues you'll need to pay, join another (non-political) club. Paying your dues means doing scut work. It also usually means being willing to climb the ladder. Whenever you get the chance, be sure your associates and allies know you're willing to put in the work. If they believe, it will show up in their support.

Paying dues also includes doing favors and asking for them in return. And it includes willingly fund-raising for yourself—but more important, perhaps, for others. Debbie Wasserman Schultz is one of the Democratic Party's biggest fund-raisers for other candidates. I've worked with individuals who thought it was beneath them to ask people less important to give money. I remind them that we all put our pants on one leg at a time and everybody's money is green. I also point out that US presidents do it all the time, and no one is more important than a president.

Are you willing to run, and run again (and again) if necessary? Debbie Wasserman Schultz started out at the age of twenty-two as a legislative aide. At twenty-six, she became the youngest woman ever elected to the Florida House of Representatives. Term-limited out after eight years, she moved over to the Florida state senate. At thirty-eight, she was elected to Congress, where she is now a chief deputy whip. In her spare time, she heads the Democratic National Committee.

Nikki Haley became a member of the South Carolina House of Representatives at the age of thirty-two. Now governor of South Carolina and the youngest governor in the United States, she ran for that office at thirty-nine. In 2012, news outlets as different as the *New York Times* and Fox News reported that her name was being tossed around as a potential vice-presidential pick for Mitt Romney.

Toni Preckwinkle had to run three times before she won her first election to the Chicago City Council. Now president of the Cook County Board of Commissioners, she runs the government of a county with a population larger than those of twenty-nine states.

If you're ready to rise despite your youth, and you're willing to start wherever you can and run as many times as it takes to get where you want to go, make sure your colleagues are in concert with you.

Are you good at building teams and appreciating the dynamics of teamwork? Are you able to think of yourself not just as team leader but as a team member? You won't be leading by divine right: you were elected or appointed to serve. So your job includes collaborating with the other waitresses.

If someone goes after you personally, are you willing to strike back? You're probably swallowing hard thinking about this one. Don't choke; remember this: during the 2012 presidential campaign, Barack Obama and Mitt Romney went at each other with charges of disingenuousness. Both were using some very fuzzy math, so maybe both were right about the other's lack of honesty. But if your opponent attacks your integrity as opposed to your facts, you'll need to be ready to do the same.

Do you love power or the idea of having it? Loving power isn't evil—if you use it for public good. On the other hand, if having power scares you, you may have a hard time using it to achieve good.

Are you willing to win only 50 percent plus 1? The availability of minute pieces of data will allow you to concentrate your campaign on very specific voter segments. There's no rule that says you have to be elected by some people from every neighborhood. Just make sure you're comfortable with the implications of a narrow victory.

Harold Washington became the first African American mayor of Chicago by beating two white opponents in the Democratic primary and later another white opponent in the general election. He was asked by the city's African American business and political leaders to run, and he agreed on the condition that those supporters would fund and organize a massive voter-registration campaign in the African American community. He told me how he was going to win the primary; he said if 95 percent of African American voters voted for him, it wouldn't matter how whites voted.

Washington knew that he'd be walking into City Hall as the mayor of a divided city. Winning election without a broad mandate makes it harder to govern. This analogy holds for appointed office as well. An overwhelming number of endorsers from the same subset may get you the appointment you desire, but you will have to build support among the other subsets in order to lead.

Are you comfortable talking about your faith in public, including how it factors into your policymaking? Are you prepared to make an argument for policy on religious grounds? Are you willing to lead religious events such as a prayer breakfast? (Which religious leaders would you invite? Which would you not? Why not?)

Are you a teacher? Three-quarters of all US teachers are women. In *Forbes* in 2012, Bryce Covert wrote that when EMILY's List, a political action committee that supports Democratic women candidates who are pro-choice, conducted focus groups with "registered, moderate, blue- or pink-collar women," it found they preferred to support "those who have an interest in community and service" instead of "career politicians or politicians who spent their lives getting rich." These community-oriented leaders include "everyday heroes, teachers, nurses, firefighters, veterans, [and] volunteers."

When Barbara Byrd-Bennett was approved by the Chicago school board as the new CEO of Chicago Public Schools, one of the most political institutions you can imagine, in October 2012, she said, "I am a teacher who happens to be the CEO." And a spokeswoman for the now-defunct White House Project, which trained women for public and business leadership, says, "We do think that the leadership assets of educators do cross over with the assets needed to run for office."

Can you find joy in a toxic environment? Your quest for public leadership takes place in a world that is often vicious. It doesn't matter whether your town's public square is big or small. Small-town, school board, and PTA politics can be as competitive and hard-hitting as those at the highest levels.

Can you take some defeat without complaint? The *New York Times* reported, "[Hillary] Clinton has little patience for those whose privilege offers them a myriad of choices but who fail to take advantage of them. 'I can't stand whining,' she says to *Marie Claire* magazine. 'I can't stand the kind of paralysis that some people fall into because they're not happy with the choices they've made. You live in a time when there are endless choices. . . . Money certainly helps, and having that kind of financial privilege goes a long way. . . . But you have to work on yourself. . . . Do something!'"

Last but not least: Do you love winning?

Just show up

Back in the late 1980s, when I was a member of the Chicago Park District's Board of Commissioners, I was invited to attend a community meeting. Barack Obama greeted me when I arrived. He was a young and ambitious organizer working on Chicago's poverty-stricken South Side, and I chaired the committee overseeing the parks' $300 million budget.

Despite what you hear about political deals being made in smoky back rooms, politics is not fundamentally a private game. Maybe you haven't been invited into a back room. So what? Politics starts with organizing people and getting them to join your team.

That's what neighborhood leaders were up to when they invited me to attend a meeting of the Developing Communities Project, and that's what I was up to when I responded that it would be my pleasure to attend.

It was a hot August night, and I was a long way from home. The invitation was for a meeting in a church basement near Altgeld Gardens, a housing project in an African American community about as far from downtown as you can go and still be in the city—speaking both geographically and figuratively. Nevertheless, I went. Not because Obama was a big deal—he wasn't then. And not because I thought I'd be hearing some new agenda for improving the parks that I hadn't heard yet or didn't agree with. I already knew the organization's wish list: like groups in every underserved neighborhood, they would want more basketball courts, more swimming pools, and a better field house. I didn't need to travel so far to learn that.

But the night had promise. I showed up. I even remember what I wore: yellow and hot pink. Why? Because this meeting would mean something in my own campaign to become a person who mattered, and I wanted to stand out.

Of course, Obama had his agenda, too. He had learned what I had: every day is Election Day.

Every single day, you're testing your ability to make your case and seeing if you can get people to buy in, whether or not there'll be any immediate return. You're convincing people that you're better for them than any alternative, and you're adding them to your network. Elections aren't all about ballots, chads, and voting booths. They're about the choices people make every day. And appointments to important political positions aren't just about qualifications. They are about the choice that people of influence have made to support and include you.

You can't win on Election Day without turnout. Turnout is getting your people where you need them to be when you need them to be there—whether it's an event, a speech, a meeting, or somewhere else you're promoting yourself. One of your major campaign objectives is selling your message and getting your people to sell it for you.

How do you ensure turnout? Well, let's take a look at that sweltering day. Of course Obama and I were both deeply committed to the improvement of our city's parks. Both of us were willing to give up an evening on behalf of a community that needed and deserved our help. But we were both ambitious, and we both knew to apply the principle of turnout in our campaigns for bigger things down the road.

Obama needed me to show up to prove he was capable of delivering a public official who would listen to his organization's concerns. He delivered such a person for his people so that they in turn would deliver for him on a future Election Day. I needed to turn out for him because I, too, was building my base. I turned out for him so he would turn out for me.

Turnout is a deceptively simple concept, yet candidates like Barack Obama spend millions to get it right. The good news is that you don't need to spend millions—you're not running for president of the United States. Yet.

If you get your people to show up for whatever constitutes that day's "poll," you will demonstrate the power of your message and your candidacy. And more important, you'll demonstrate your personal power. Everyday occasions like school or community fund-raisers or even celebrations for friends or family can show your ability to spread a message and use it to precipitate action.

Taking the necessary time—in advance—to create awareness of the event across the widest applicable universe of people will make a huge difference in your success.

And people like to be included. I can't even count the number of times I've sent invitations asking for something and still gotten sincere responses saying, "Thanks for including me." This doesn't always happen, but politics is a percentage game. To get some votes, you have to ask for a lot. And the more you ask for, the more you'll probably get.

If politics is about percentages, turnout is about volume. The more frequently you send your invitations, thank the people who turned out, and send follow-up invitations, the more turnout you'll get, and the more your successes will speak to your likelihood of winning on future Election Days.

These repeated contacts will help build loyalty for the long haul. Everyone you reach is also a future constituent, which will protect you after Election Day when times get tough, as they always do. Your new advocates will help you win again.

And there's another group you need to turn out for. Politicians joke about the rubber-chicken circuit, but there's no greater imperative in politics than showing up for the other guy. Your visible commitment to the work of others is the political application of the Golden Rule, and nothing carries more weight than showing up—because if you don't show up for them, they won't show up for you.

In Chicago, your precinct captain calls you on Election Day to make sure you intend to vote. If you can't make it to the polling place on your own, someone will come by to drive you. And when that level of organization fails—as it can, even in Chicago—opportunities open up for others who can bring in the votes.

Of course, your positions on issues matter. But I'm talking about the gap between what should happen and what does happen. Without turnout, there's only defeat.

Now that you get the concept, it's time to apply it. Keep reading to see how.

Strategic imperatives for showing up and making your presence count:

★ Reach out to your present and potential constituents systematically and frequently.

★ Develop personal relationships with as many of the leaders of each constituency as you can.

★ Once you've developed those relationships, show up for each of those leaders as often as you can.

★ Invite them to ask you to turn out for the colleagues who are important to them.

★ Press repeat.

5

Every act creates ripples

When you're imagining a public career, you're dreaming big and then planning big. At the same time, each small act will matter. People don't remember what you did, but they do remember how you made them feel, no matter when, no matter where, and no matter how small the circumstance. The ripples extend far into the distance.

Join lots of organizations and causes so that you create ripples in lots of ponds. Before you know it, those ponds become lakes, and those lakes become oceans. And the earlier you get started, the better. People who aren't willing to bust their butts don't really want to win.

Laura Tucker serves on the board of directors of the Planned Parenthood Action Fund, the political arm of the Planned Parenthood Federation of America. She is an excellent model for how to become a bigger fish, creating ever bigger ripples in ever bigger ponds. Tucker is the stepdaughter of the late James B. Moran, who was a lawyer when he and Tucker's mother married. Moran had been a member of the city council of Evanston, Tucker's hometown in the Chicago suburbs, and a member of the Illinois House of Representatives, all before being appointed to the US District Court, Northern District of Illinois. Tucker learned politics at the feet of a master.

While still in college, Tucker worked as a field organizer for Walter Mondale's campaign for the presidency in 1984. In successive presidential campaigns, she became a delegate tracker, an advance person, and, just eight years after her start, a regional director of operations for the 1992 Clinton-Gore campaign. After their election, she parlayed her experience into the opportunity to create the nation's first women's advocacy division in a state attorney general's office and, later, into directing a bipartisan project to recruit, train, and elect progressive candidates to the Illinois state legislature. Along the way, she became a volunteer fund-raiser and a major political donor herself to federal candidates all over the nation.

Tucker is savvy about consolidating her responsibilities (and power) so that the bigger ripples can be created sooner rather than later. She's a longtime devoted member of the board of directors of the Chicago Foundation for Women, which raises and grants millions of dollars every year to women's causes. She has chaired two of its most important committees: the fund-raising committee and the grant-making committee. As chair of the fund-raising committee, she met wealthy donors. As chair of the grant-making committee, she met leaders of organizations all over the city. Recently, Tucker was a member of the foundation's presidential search committee, giving her a direct say in the foundation's future.

Tucker's consolidation of her power means she's got precinct workers in every neighborhood where she needs voters for herself and her causes, including that oh-so-valuable one for would-be girl-politicos, the one where rich women who care about women's issues live. Wealthy women have become Tucker's friends, creating ever bigger ponds for Tucker to swim in.

If you're interested in politics and public leadership, be valuable to organizations that champion women's political causes and support lots of candidates with your time. Then work hard raising money for them. And don't ever worry about spreading yourself too thin.

Another strategy for creating bigger ripples in bigger ponds is to identify yourself with a particular issue or cause. The attention will enable you to seek public support, which then can be converted to public power. When Hillary Clinton moved to Arkansas—instead of to Wall Street—after marrying Bill Clinton, she might have been in a fix: her ambition matched his; but many considered Arkansas a backwater, and she was unknown there. Looking around, Clinton converted her ambition for public leadership into advocacy for low-income children and their families. As a result, when she became a member of the board of directors of the Children's Defense Fund, she achieved national recognition for her commitment, one of constant interest to national policy makers and politicians.

When I ask successful women how carefully they planned their route to power, most say not so much. Instead, they say, their power and influence came from their dedication to becoming really knowledgeable and working really hard. So, like Clinton and Tucker, work hard, be generous, and be nice. But don't bother to swim in small ponds that don't flow into big lakes.

Strategic imperatives for becoming a big fish:

★ Be willing to start small. Minnows grow.

★ Identify the political masters in your community, work for and learn from them, and figure out how to emulate their success.

★ Identify the organizations and campaigns that will serve you and your campaign best. Join them.

★ Become somebody who matters in every one of those organizations by working as strategically and enthusiastically as you can.

★ Cheerfully take on the responsibilities of leadership.

★ Adopt this attitude: I can organize anything—just ask me. I'm willing to help raise money—just ask me. I go to meetings all the time—I love them. I can make the case for you—just ask me. When I go on to bigger things, I'll remember you. Just test me.

6

Size does matter

When it comes to winning on Election Day, size matters *a lot*. You need to have more support than the other girl—there is absolutely no substitute for numbers. But size matters in every other corner of the political playing field as well, and usually bigger is better. There's the size of your commitment, the size of your personal investment in helping others, the size of your fortitude and how you'll handle obstacles, the size of your expertise and skill, the size of your reputation and visibility, the size of your personal network, the stature of your supporters, the size of your heart, and the size of your willingness to work your way up the ladder, no matter how many rungs there are.

In 2009, Hillary Clinton left her Senate seat to serve in the cabinet of President Barack Obama. New York governor David Paterson appointed US representative Kirsten Gillibrand to replace her, choosing Gillibrand over contenders with bigger media presences and better political resumés. She won the first-term seat again in a special election held in 2010 and a second term in 2012.

The daughter of two attorneys, Gillibrand has been actively encouraging women to move into the foreground in politics, to relinquish their traditional roles in the background—following the example of her grandmother Dorothea "Polly" Noonan, who was an operative in the Democratic political machine in Albany, New York, and founded the Albany Democratic Women's Club. In 2011, Gillibrand founded an organization called Off the Sidelines, which urges women to get involved in the issues they care about because, as she says on her 2012 campaign website, "Women have the power to shape the future. It's just a matter of getting off the sidelines and getting involved." Off the Sidelines engages women all over the country, providing access to resources for women who want to be political activists and run for office. Gillibrand is a US senator now, but if she has higher ambitions, a by-product of her work on this cause is that she's building awareness of herself and growing a large national potential constituency. No matter what she wants to achieve, the bigger the size of her constituency, the better.

Carol Moseley Braun is the only African American woman to ever win a seat in the US Senate. Her first election was to the Illinois House of Representatives. After nine years there, she ran for Cook County recorder of deeds. She won and served in that office until she ran for the US Senate in 1992. While it's not clear why the recorder of deeds position is even an elected one, because its duties are administrative, holding the office keeps the incumbent off the sidelines and in front of the voters. It certainly served that purpose for Moseley Braun. In 1992, when there was an opening for a candidate in the Illinois Democratic Party primary for the US Senate, there Braun was: in the public eye, a proven vote getter, able to use the platform and visibility of her current office to boost her to the next.

Whether you're trying to work your way up the office ladder or win election to the highest office in the land, you'll campaign for any position or office that will help you get there. Don't get hung up on the size of the intermediate office.

Monica Banks had an outsized dream and figured out early on that it was going to take a big plan to achieve it. An African American Democrat in Oktibbeha County in Mississippi—a state whose voters are increasingly Republican—she is the only African American holding city- or countywide office, and the first woman in more than forty years to win the office of chancery clerk. She's now been reelected five times, running unopposed in 2011 and winning each race by a larger margin.

I was introduced to Banks by Derrick Johnson, president of the Mississippi NAACP. He said I would be inspired and impressed, and he was right. Banks grew up outside of Maben, Mississippi, which has a population of less than 1,000. Her newly desegregated high school was bombed shortly before she arrived. During Career Day in eleventh grade, Banks saw the circuit court clerk give a talk and got the idea to run for the office herself someday. Banks says, "She was a very classy lady, very smart, candid and direct." Banks knew she enjoyed clerical work and wanted to help people in her career; the job of circuit clerk sounded like a good fit.

Banks began by studying business administration in high school and junior college and then at Mississippi State University. At the same time, she began volunteering for the local Democratic Party and NAACP chapter, and she was befriended by Dr. Douglas Conner, its president, who had delivered Banks in her grandfather's country home. Banks left Mississippi State to work in a local law firm. But her community political work continued.

After a dozen years of volunteering for campaigns and developing substantial political know-how, she was invited to run a campaign for a white woman who was running as a long-shot candidate for state senator against a white man, the preferred candidate of the party establishment. "You're just the one to get her grassroots movement going," said the state representative who recruited her. Banks coordinated her first campaign: "Dad-gummit, we beat him," she says.

Banks was occasionally asked to run against the circuit clerk, though she repeatedly declined. When the clerk finally announced her retirement, Banks thought her moment had arrived. But then another political activist came to see her, announcing her intention to run and asking for her support. "It hurt me to my heart," says Banks, "but I turned that dream loose there and then. For some reason, I could not deny her. But later I understood. God had other plans for me. I liked His plan better than mine." Banks knew what she wanted, but this race wasn't going to be it.

Banks got lucky the following week. The local newspaper announced that the county's chancery clerk, after thirty-five years in office, was resigning as well. The job wasn't the one she had been dreaming of all those years, but it was an important public office none-theless, requiring the same business and administrative skills she had spent years honing, so she decided to go for it. Banks called on people in her religious community, in the Democratic Party, and in NAACP leadership and asked for their support. She also called on friends she knew in business, including the white attorney she worked for at the time and people she knew through his office: "In this predominantly white community, the crossover white vote was crucial to my win-ning my election. He didn't miss a beat. He said: 'Go for it.'" And she pounded the pavement: "I like the door-to-door better than getting up on the political stump," she says. She asked them all to endorse her and become part of what she was now thinking of as her "movement."

"I was trying to capture my dream, not to prove anything to the world." She won by twenty-three votes.

The lines you will need to cross to build your movement may be racial or professional or social. In this context, less is never more. You'll need to build a big and diverse base, and then keep on adding to it. As your snowball of support builds, it will gather its own weight, and when it's big enough, it will roll down the hill to victory.

There are all sorts of ways to add to your snowball, depending on your interests and personal strengths. You can become a Girl Scout leader, or an advocate for victims of violence, or a Career Day speaker. Big efforts will demonstrate your aptitude for public leadership.

Strategic imperatives on how to achieve the biggest possible sphere of influence:

★ Take on projects and join interest groups outside your campaign.

★ Walk every precinct.

★ Because your base will grow incrementally, start with the bigger precincts.

★ Solve other people's problems, focusing on those that a lot of people may have.

★ Create relationships with supporters who have big bases of their own.

7

Bankroll yourself with whatever you've got; then ask others to bank on you

I once knew a candidate with substantial means she was unwilling to use on her own campaign—any of it. But she had no problem asking others to pull out their checkbooks on her behalf. She felt she was on a worthy mission and that those who shared her goals could put up the cash while she gave her time. I could never figure out why she thought others should invest in her when she wasn't willing to do the same. What did that say about her campaign? Well, it said, "You lose," as it turns out.

Money isn't the only way to invest in yourself so others will do the same. This chapter describes the investments you can make, and a couple of Chicago friends of mine supply good examples.

The success story of Ertharin Cousin, executive director of the United Nations World Food Programme, involves that wonderful renewable resource: sweat equity. Cousin's family migrated to Chicago from Louisiana, and she grew up in Lawndale, a poor African American neighborhood on Chicago's West Side. She graduated from the University of Illinois's Chicago campus, just a few miles away from her childhood home, without funds but with lots to contribute. After law school, Cousin got a thorough political schooling in a succession of jobs with the Illinois attorney general, with Chicago mayor Harold Washington, and in the AT&T government relations department. Then Bill Clinton came calling.

Cousin was hired as a staffer in the first Clinton-Gore presidential campaign in 1992, became an official at the Democratic National Committee, and was an appointee on the State Department's Board for International Food and Agricultural Development.

After working for the Clinton administration, Cousin went to work in the private sector, serving as executive in charge of government relations for Albertson's, one of the nation's largest supermarket chains. She also joined the board of America's Second Harvest (now Feeding America), the nation's largest antihunger organization. Later she joined the agency's staff, coordinating its response to the devastation of New Orleans by Hurricane Katrina.

Are you sweating yet? But you already knew that winning your election would require hard work. What's important about Cousin's story is how she converted all this sweat into equity as valuable as cash. For more than two decades, she built and maintained connections with people she met along the way, working to help their fortunes rise, utilizing both her technical skills and her substantive knowledge in a variety of jobs across both the private and public sectors. She was willing to uproot herself geographically in order to help out, and she was loyal to whomever brought her to the dance.

She also has stuck with an issue she cares about. In 2012, when former US senator and presidential candidate George McGovern entered hospice care, Cousin posted a link on Facebook to South Dakota food pantries as a tribute. Perhaps this kind of care, as well as her hard work, accounts for her place on *Forbes* magazine's 2012 list of the most powerful women in the world.

Cousin hit the ground running at twenty-five, with nothing in hand but her degrees. Thirty years later she was appointed executive director of the United Nations World Food Programme. Despite her humble beginnings (she told her UN colleagues that until the day he died, her father couldn't spell her name), Cousin has lived in the chief of mission's residence in Rome as the US ambassador to the United Nations World Food Programme and will always be entitled to the honorific "ambassador"; the budget she now manages is in the neighborhood of $7 billion. Talking to Mississippi Delta–born *Chicago Sun-Times* reporter Mary Mitchell, she said, "I believe that you can do anything. But it starts with you. Working hard, studying, ensuring that you graduate from high school, and seeing college not as a way to get a job, but the way to build opportunity." A bankroll, you might say. This incredible life story appeared in Mitchell's column under the headline "She manages her hair by keeping it simple"!

Rachel Durchslag is active in social justice causes as well; but she was born into wealth, and she's used her personal good fortune to advance causes for women. Several years ago, Durchslag founded the Chicago Alliance Against Sexual Exploitation: "Ending harm, demanding change." In the process, Durchslag bankrolled herself into the national limelight.

A decade ago, after she received her graduate degree in social service administration, Durchslag says she saw a film about sex trafficking and afterward wondered, "What would it be like to experience daily rape?" After she "applied for a lot of jobs and didn't get them," she traveled to Thailand to "work with young women who had been kidnapped or sold into the sex trade."

Back in Chicago, Durchslag says, "I was able to realize my own vision. This was a way to legitimize what I was already doing. I thought people would take me more seriously if I had a business card. I set up my office and started making connections." Her agenda was to "end demand," conduct public education, develop and disseminate curricula, advocate for legislative and policy reform, and engage in civil litigation "against perpetrators and facilitators of sexual harm."

Admittedly, Durchslag enjoys the luxury of being able to do work that she finds meaningful. She says, "I like to feel I have value—that people take me seriously because I want to make change." And she's lucky she can afford the time off she has made a part of her daily life. "I wanted to have flexibility to teach and to travel when I wanted to." Just another girl doing her thing because she can afford to? Not exactly—her position of privilege is allowing her to give enormous aid to women much less privileged than she.

Lisa Bourdeaux Percy, who began working as a White House staffer for Jimmy Carter at age twenty-three and later worked for Mississippi governor Ray Mabus, seems to personify the expression "steel magnolia." She married into one of the largest of the Mississippi Delta's plantation-owning families. The author Walker Percy may be the best-known member of that family, but Walker Percy's cousins, the "farmers," as they refer to themselves, were among those who ruled the Delta with private wealth and public power, including her husband's grandfather, US senator LeRoy Percy.

But Lisa Bordeaux came to the marriage and the Percys' ancestral home in Greenville, "Queen City of the Delta," with her own political pedigree. Her mother, Norma Bourdeaux, was a Mississippi state representative for two terms in the 1990s, running for office for the first time at age sixty-one. Bourdeaux served on the second grand jury (there were two) in the case of slain civil rights workers James Chaney, Andrew Goodman, and Michael Schwerner, who were lynched during the Freedom Summer of 1964 in Neshoba County, Mississippi. According to Lisa, her mother was horrified to hear that an unindicted coconspirator in the killings was running for office. "Oh no. He can't represent me," she said, and she decided to run against him.

Daughter followed in mother's footsteps, working in the state government as a lobbyist, which is where she met her husband, Billy Percy. Lisa Percy loved her work and was one of few women lobbyists at the time. After marrying, the Percys moved to Greenville. While there, Percy drafted state legislation to create a building fund for the arts and lobbied successfully for its passage. She volunteers without pay for public causes, including for candidates and advocacy projects. Her fellow board members recently elected her as secretary of the Delta Health Alliance. Percy says she told the men when they elected her, "The only reason I'm taking this job is because the fellow who is now the president was the secretary before me."

Percy is donating time and cash to her career. She's also helping bankroll daughters of sharecroppers at those plantations into public leadership.

Like Ertharin Cousin and the steel magnolias in the movie of the same name, Donna Brazile hails from Louisiana. She grew up in Kenner, the third child of nine in a poor if upstanding family. "My mama taught me to play by the rules and respect those rules," she said to a Democratic National Committee colleague. Her father was a Korean War veteran with four bronze medals and a United Nations Medal of Valor. When he passed away, it was said, "He was decent, kind . . . tough as nails, extremely generous, compassionate, and fearless."

Brazile first became interested in politics as a child, and in high school she participated in Upward Bound, which offers college scholarships to low-income students. By age twenty-five, she was acting on the national political stage. In 1984, she was a senior member of the presidential campaign staff of Jesse Jackson Sr.

In 2000, Brazile, age forty-one, became Al Gore's presidential campaign manager, the first African American and only the second woman to direct a major party presidential campaign. Between 1984 and 2000, Brazile had worked in other Democratic presidential campaigns and as chief of staff to representative Eleanor Holmes Norton of Washington, DC.

Brazile bankrolled her political career with a combination of other people's money and her own discipline and grit, capitalizing on meeting and befriending people of means or access to means, and developing powerful mentors. Figuratively, Brazile is "stirring the pots in America" (the subtitle of her autobiography, *Cooking with Grease*), sharing her story of how to bootstrap oneself into political power and influence.

By age twenty-eight, I had run the statewide media campaign for International Women's Year, started a women's center, and written a guide to women's services in Chicago, and I was the fund-raiser and media person for the National Women's Political Caucus campaign to ratify the Equal Rights Amendment (ERA) in Illinois. The National Women's Political Caucus had recruited celebrities to lobby for the

ERA and major donors to fund its lobbying, media, and public education programs to promote ratification. Carol Burnett, Marlo Thomas,
senator Charles Percy, Christie Hefner, and Ann Landers all signed on.
My charge was to engage them. In a sense, I was bankrolling my own
start in politics. I developed relationships with individuals who became
my supporters when I founded a women's issues advocacy coalition.

Bank robber Willie Sutton said he robbed banks because that's
where the money was. Political fund-raisers ask rich people for money
because that's where the money is. In the process, they build a network
that can be leveraged for the public good. Your task is to identify what
bills are in your bankroll, create a bigger bankroll, and always spend
it wisely.

Strategic imperatives for bankrolling your campaign:

★ Give. A contribution of any kind—money, time, connections—creates a debt. When you spend, you will receive.

★ Record your contributions.

★ Make contributions frequently.

★ Keep track of those who like the kind of giving you do, and get to
  know them.

★ Give again.

8

Become a fund-raiser

In politics as in so many other professions, there is a push to focus on one area of expertise. Lawyers typically specialize. Doctors do, too. Even those whose goal is to run large businesses choose some aspect of the business with which to make their mark as they climb the corporate ladder. Politics works the same way. If you start out as a staffer and you're smart, you will happily do whatever you're told to do. But as you achieve success, you'll have the opportunity to select a specialty. Likewise, when you volunteer for a leadership role in a political campaign, or decide to seek public office yourself, you will have the opportunity to develop expertise in an area and be appreciated for that expertise. However, no matter what area you become a specialist in, you'll always need to become a fund-raiser, too. Here are some reasons why.

Everyone needs money. Say you're running to be a school board member or township officer. You're going to want yard signs and fliers to distribute at meetings and as you walk door to door. Those cost money. If you demonstrate your ability to raise the money to print those signs and fliers, you'll prove you are a problem solver of a very useful kind, the kind who can find money to fund worthy causes. That's something voters and other leaders appreciate.

Fund-raising shows you're serious. Take those yard signs and fliers: the printing bill is small, but you don't have the money to pay it. Do you give up and say no to yard signs and fliers? Not a chance. You will ask however many friends and family members you need to contribute a portion of the cost. Or ask your loyal customers or clients if they will each pay a share. Or hold a bake sale or a carwash, or host a pancake dinner, fish fry, or dinner dance. Or stage a walk or motorcycle ride, a pig roast, or, my new favorite, a chicken-noodle-soup fund-raiser. The possibilities for raising money are infinite. If you don't explore them, you're not serious.

Fund-raising is the fastest and most methodical way to get to know everyone you need to know and want to know. To fund the printing of those yard signs and fliers, you're going to have to decide who to ask (see above). This exercise will force you to evaluate each potential donor's interest in giving. Not only that, the exercise will also force you to rank people in order of contact because you want to raise this money as fast as possible, in order to get the yard signs and fliers out there as soon as possible. You could decide not to research and rank people, but why wouldn't you if you're serious about winning (and therefore willing to put in the time needed)? This information will hold you in good stead the next time you need yard signs and fliers, or to fund some other expense. And the more often you exercise this way, the more fit you will become.

Asking for money hones your messaging and sales skills. What is your argument? People don't give just because you ask. You have to develop and make a clear case. It will need to state a compelling combination of reasons why those yard signs and fliers are a good idea. It will need to demonstrate how you will use those signs and fliers strategically. It will need to demonstrate that you are planning to spend the right amount of money on purchasing them (not too many, not too few; not getting too fancy, but nice enough). Once you've developed your case for the yard signs and fliers, and you've contextualized it in your larger message about why you're running in the first place (that's the message you'll be printing on the yard signs and fliers), you will be good to go—now and forever—as a politician. Because you know how to sell yourself and your cause.

Proposing to spend other people's money induces budgetary discipline and creativity. I can't tell you how many times I've seen four-color fliers when two-color would have done just fine. Or yard signs with lots of color but type so small you can't read the message. Perhaps those candidates were only spending their own money. But you're not. Consequently, you want to fund as much activity as you can with as few dollars as possible.

This commitment to the prudent use of other people's money will induce creativity on your part. Will the printer do the work for you at cost, or at cost-plus but not full freight? Will the printer contribute the design time and only charge you for the hard printing costs? The same kind of discipline and creativity you apply to getting your yard signs and fliers printed can be applied to all your budget's line items, no matter their size.

Fund-raising puts you in the rooms where decisions are made. When you solicit a larger-than-average contribution, or one that's large in absolute terms, odds are you will be soliciting someone with decision-making influence or power in your community. That person might be the printer, business colleagues you ask to fund a share of the printing bill, or friends who are 'school board members you ask to participate in your bake sale. Decision-making community leaders typically have money themselves or access to it. For example, think bankers; car and equipment dealers; and owners of grocery stores, gas stations, convenience stores, and large farms. You will meet to make the ask in person. You will talk about the weather or the soccer team or the latest political news. Don't ever try to make this ask over the phone. That would make it even easier to back out after the talk about the weather. Sit in that person's space and get to know how she presents and thinks. Make her feel sufficiently comfortable to consider investing in you. Ask her to invest. Once she does, I guarantee she will invite you back. You are on your way.

Fund-raising gives you stature. Your success in getting others to fund you makes you somebody who matters. Even the most wealthy or generous donors don't decide to give lightly. They consider each gift in the same way they consider any financial investment: Does this company/person have value because it/she produces something I value? Is that value sustainable? Is that value capable of being increased? Once these questions have been answered with a yes, you'll get your check. And you'll get the stature that derives from being a person of proven value. Then you can utilize that newfound stature in all kinds of contexts that matter to your Election Day plans and dreams.

Successful fund-raising demonstrates you have a constituency. Donations satisfy multiple goals. You've funded an expense. You've built a set of donors that can be asked to fund future expenses. You now know generous people who probably associate with others who are also generous who can now be tapped by you. You've proved you're not tilting at windmills and you're not a lone ranger. You've demonstrated that you are leading a movement, or at least driving the bandwagon. You appear to be the front-runner, which will enable you to broaden your message and talk like a winner. And once you start talking like a winner, the press will report on you that way. This all started with asking for money.

Your ability to raise money will put you at the center of others' worlds. Pretty much everyone needs money. Therefore, pretty much everyone will include you. Growing up, I heard the line "money talks, nobody walks" delivered by WABC Radio announcer Charlie Greer to promote an area clothing store. When I became a fund-raiser in my twenties, that line jumped to mind. It's never left. That's because it is a great metaphor for the significance of fund-raising. Your fund-raising will put everybody in suits, no matter how modest the make or the cut. Literally, the money you raise means you will have the resources to obtain a position to advocate for better parks or schools or playgrounds, or for buying better books and gym equipment. Way better than a new suit. Nobody's walking. Everybody's riding high.

Fund-raising opens doors like nothing else. When you're ready to move on up from the school board, say, your donors will share helpful information with you, because you have used their money wisely. (See that earlier list of decision-maker types.) They may know of opportunities you don't. Perhaps there is a state job your school board experience qualifies you for. Perhaps there is a county appointment you didn't think was realistic to consider. Now, it will be.

Fund-raising makes you a broker of a scarce and valuable commodity: access to important people. Even if this access is in a meeting or your fund-raising event, it's bound to be more intimate than the auditorium where the speech will be delivered. That access enables you to be in the know about important or juicy info (though what's important is usually juicy anyway). That sharing creates the appearance of power and influence, just what you as a candidate who needs to raise money always needs to have. This access also enables you to share your views about important events in your community directly with those who make decisions about it. In this context, you are a player of the best sort.

It's incredible how much people will help you once you maneuver yourself into the broker position. For instance, a person you don't know well will respond positively to your request to write a big check. Even if the next time you call her, she is "out of town" (because she doesn't need to meet that person for whom you are raising money), you still have a relationship with her.

When I was a star Girl Scout, I was terrible at selling Girl Scout cookies. I just didn't believe that selling cookies was central to being a Girl Scout, so I wasn't motivated. I thought, Salesperson, me? No way.

Girl, was I wrong. A decade later, when I was selling the idea of building a women's center, I was a big success. That's because there was a clear connection for me between raising funds for the women's center and the good it would do for the women and girls of Chicago.

Think about your fund-raising for your—or others'—candidacies in the same context: You need that money to do right by your community. You would be remiss if you didn't ask for it. Be a fund-raiser. Stay a fund-raiser. Learn fund-raising strategy and techniques (see the "Resources" section on page 197). As your public career grows, hire fund-raising staffers in order to increase your bankroll.

Strategic imperatives for becoming a fund-raising dynamo:

★ Hold a bake sale.

★ Figure out how your budget can be met in the least amount of time and with the fewest donors. Then work back from that math to determine what's practical in terms of gift size among your likely donors.

★ Create a message those donors will like.

★ Develop and execute a plan to engage donors that connects to the message you are sending. For instance, if your message is about diverse community engagement, make sure your donors are from diverse constituencies.

★ When you commit to becoming a fund-raiser, learn all the types of sales approaches and tactics. Those for big sales, those for little sales. Those where volume matters most (to show size of constituency). Those where you're looking for one big get: I need that billboard now.

★ Understand the connections among your donors as a baseline for expanding their number.

★ Take the initiative in introducing your donors to one another. This will be self-reinforcing for them and is a good strategy for encouraging them to become leaders on your behalf, because the introduction will validate their connection to you.

★ Hold a bigger bake sale.

9

Create your brand; make it stand out

Voters don't get excited about the business-as-usual type who slumps about in Casual Friday slacks and sensible shoes. Campaigning with distinctive style and flair will underscore your other special quality: your willingness to stand up for yourself and stick to your platform. Don't be afraid to be different. Remember Michelle Obama's bare arms and Condoleezza Rice's high-heeled black boots? If you can similarly stake your claim to a look, you'll stake your claim to a little part of the voters' memory and become a distinctive brand voters never forget.

Think about the last time you watched the State of the Union address. First Lady Nancy Reagan wore a red suit. Since then, red has never lost its position as the political power color of choice. Don't get me wrong—red packs a punch. But it loses some impact when everyone's wearing it. You don't want to be just another face in the crowd.

Judge Ilana D. Rovner walked up to me at an event where I was wearing purple. She said, "Rebecca, do you know that purple is the color of royalty?" I sure did. Rovner was wearing purple that day, too. She would be thought special, even if not royal. She would stand out in the crowd. She would be remembered for her presence as well as her talent and accomplishment. "Always wear it," she said. Actually, I often do.

The other option is black, assuming you're not in a crowd of men at a funeral. The day I met Gwen Page, superintendent of schools in Mississippi's East Jasper School District, she was impeccably dressed in a sharp black suit, carrying an oversized Louis Vuitton bag, and wearing very high heels. But for much of her early adult life, Page didn't need to dress up to stand out. Raised as a child working in a cotton field, she earned a PhD by the age of thirty. Page says, "I can just hear my mom telling me, 'People perceive you how you present yourself.' There is no such thing as mediocrity if you want to catapult yourself to the top." And she started standing out early. An African American, she attended Mississippi Delta Community College (MDCC), where the student body is primarily white. At MDCC, she was vice president of the student government association, a clarinetist in the marching band, a member of the yearbook staff, and a member of Delta Connection (a public relations team). Page received her BS in microbiology from Mississippi University for Women, where she was an avid volunteer with Big Brothers Big Sisters of America. She earned her PhD in educational leadership and administration at Mississippi State University, where she was inducted into Alpha Theta Thi collegiate honor society.

When Page attended MDCC, she was Miss Mississippi Delta Community College, the first African American woman awarded this honor. She was also a member of the Delta Dancers—at the time, one of only three African American members. (They're still in the minority twenty years later.) Membership in the Delta Dancers is highly competitive, because each member receives a scholarship for full tuition and room and board. (Page thought her chances of being picked were slim: "I just saw a sign that said 'Dance scholarship.' I just said, 'Shucks, the worst they can tell me is no.'") But they told her yes, and Page became a standout all over town. The Delta Dancers appear at football and basketball games, at pep rallies, at community events, in parades, and in a special spring revue.

Page says that when she became the first African American Miss Mississippi Delta Community College, the honor "helped to redefine my view of the world. Junior college changed everything for me. You can do anything. You can be anything." She says, "I thought [until then] all whites were racist. I chopped cotton [for white plantation owners] starting at the age of eight." We're talking the 1980s here.

At Mississippi University for Women, which says it "provides a high quality liberal arts education with a distinct emphasis on professional development and leadership opportunities for women," Page was also a standout. She was a member of Beta Beta Beta, the national honor society for college biology students, and of Alpha Epsilon Delta, a national honor society for pre-med students. After graduation, she became a leader of other kinds: teacher, curriculum director, assistant superintendent, school superintendent.

Mississippi has elected more African Americans to public office than any other state, and many of those officials are women. Derrick Johnson, president of the Mississippi NAACP, pointed out to me that school superintendent is one of the most politically sensitive jobs around. He is right. You report to an elected body that may have little professional expertise but has firm opinions about what is right for the students. You must be accessible yet remain an authority figure. You have no professional peers among your coworkers. And your daily decisions about what's best for your community are circumscribed by statewide rules that, by their very nature, can't take into account local variations in culture and demography. The job needs someone who's willing to stand out from the crowd.

As I thought about the way Page catapulted herself to the top, I kept returning to the fact that she was a cheerleader and a dancer. In those roles, you literally stand out. While Page's willingness to stand out from the crowd in word and deed is what makes her story worth sharing, you also don't forget she is in the room. I think this is helpful to her.

The same thing is true when you run a chain of reproductive health clinics. That job belonged to another southern woman, Susan Hill, and she chose it for herself. After the US Supreme Court ruled in *Roe v. Wade* that abortion is a constitutionally protected medical procedure, Hill started the National Women's Health Organization, which opened health clinics in a number of places, including Jackson, Mississippi.

As young women, Hill and I knew each other well. We were both members of the Board of Directors of NARAL, then the National Abortion Rights Action League. It's now NARAL Pro-Choice America. At those NARAL board meetings, two women in attendance didn't dress like the others. One was yours truly. The other was Susan Hill. After she died, another colleague wrote, "When she walked into a room, she literally lit up the place. . . . I still have a picture in my mind of Susan, in high heels and short skirt, standing defiantly in front of the doorway of her Fort Wayne clinic facing hundreds of protesters."

Hill was a knockout: bottle-blonde, shoulder-length hair; heavy eye makeup; a fabulous figure; fantastic clothes that were always just a little too rich and a little too evening for daytime business. But she wanted to stand out. She seemed always to be going to great parties.

Of course, being stunning is not a prerequisite to success, but being remembered is. No one ever forgot meeting Susan Hill. That helped her do her job. That's the advice Judge Rovner gave me. Don't let them forget they met you. Wearing purple will be your insurance policy.

First Lady Michelle Obama has used her wardrobe as a calling card even while seeming to play it down. She is known in the fashion press and women's magazines for not releasing information about the designers of her outfits. Reporters have to dig for the information that fashion groupies like me crave and the mystery adds to the excitement. It's clear Obama spends a lot of time figuring out what to wear. For instance, Obama changed her look during the course of the 2008 presidential campaign, when the president's advisers told her she needed to soften her public image.

Out with the suits we used to see her wearing in Chicago, in with the cardigans and circle skirts—a little more June Cleaver, a little less Clair Huxtable. Then she switched it up again when she arrived at the White House. Her bare arms were everywhere, including at her husband's first State of the Union. No red suit for her.

Maybe Obama decided to celebrate her sense of self once she was at the White House. She couldn't hold a job or express her views on anything much, after all. She would be everything the First Lady is supposed to be: a loving wife and mother, a woman who is charitable and kind to strangers, a champion of noncontroversial causes, a woman who holds hands with her husband and is never seen standing in front of him. At the same time, her bare arms allowed her to assert her own power. I loved it. I still do. When we think of her, we think power.

When Gwen Page was describing her intense, constant interaction with her school board, she said, "You have to find your own voice. . . . Be comfortable with who you are and know what you believe, what you stand for. . . . Be comfortable in your own skin; be a risk taker but be prepared for the consequences." Bare arms, sharp suits, and high heels help.

Strategic imperatives for becoming a distinctive brand:

★ Identify your best characteristics as early in your career as you can, and then refine your presentation based on those characteristics. The sum total will be your brand.

★ Identify your best physical feature, the one that will draw attention away from the ones that aren't so hot. Then emphasize it. Looking good counts.

★ Willingness to be different can demonstrate self-confidence. Consider this truth as you develop your brand's distinctive qualities.

★ If you decide to go the "cloth coat sanctimony" route, make sure you keep to that straight and narrow; the more sanctimonious you are, the harder and farther you will fall if you veer off message.

★ Write a simple declarative sentence that describes you as you wish to be described. Write the sentence so that it trips off the tongue with positives even your opposition has to say fairly describe you. (Then, if she doesn't, you get to rebut.)

10

You'll always be fighting for shelf space, so make sure you're a premium brand

Competition is high for positions of public leadership. Always present yourself as someone who brings the best blend of passion, leadership, vision, and the desire to serve. You are a premium brand, deserving of prominent shelf space and constant customer loyalty.

Former secretary of state Hillary Clinton, a woman who clearly possesses healthy doses of all of the above, has suffered some blows that would make many run for cover, not for the world stage. Every one of us is flawed, and every one of us has personal associations with other flawed people, be they spouses who stray, partners who behave badly, or family members with problematic business associates. But Clinton proves that as long as you maintain your own integrity, working hard and making smart choices along the way, your brand can become a top seller.

Frances Beinecke, president of the Natural Resources Defense Council (NRDC) and one of three members of the commission appointed by President Obama to investigate the BP Deepwater Horizon oil spill, has become a premium brand, and she uses her status to advocate for the public good—relentlessly. Under her leadership, NRDC, whose purpose is "to safeguard the Earth: its people, its plants and animals and the natural systems on which all life depends," has been an unsparing critic of the powerful, including politicians and business leaders who oppose this mission or are thinking about opposing it. For instance, NRDC was a leader in the campaign to pressure President Obama not to authorize the Keystone pipeline. Beinecke's calls to NRDC members to contact Obama were insistent but consistent with the advice for winning that she shared with me: "Respect others and demand respect in return. Have a constant willingness to take on the responsibilities of leadership, always making all others feel comfortable around you. Understand the worldwide web of connections, in order to use them to promote a good cause."

When John Adams, founding president of NRDC, retired, he recommended that Beinecke take his place. Through a succession of tough assignments, such as serving as executive director and leading the agency's strategic planning process, Beinecke had become the political leader NRDC needed next. Beinecke ran, in a manner of speaking, unopposed that Election Day. Beinecke says that while anger can be a motivating force in working for the public good, people trust her and the organization: "We are smart, credible, and responsible. People look at us and know they will get a well-thought-out, balanced reaction. We'll sit down and figure it out—what the result could be—instead of going from left field." And because of their consistent and measured approach, they are regarded as "tough." They have built a premium brand.

If you have your facts straight and take the time to understand what the other person wants, you'll have a chance of solving the problem, even when you are disagreeing with the president. Beinecke says, "You can be polite but strong. You can be respectful of the position of the presidency but critical of the action, not the person, in order to move that person to a better position."

Catherine D. Kimball, chief justice of the Louisiana Supreme Court from 2009 to February 1, 2013, knows that being a judge requires intelligence, thoughtfulness, and hard work. But those are just the basics.

What makes you a premium brand is being willing to do whatever it takes to get the job done. After Hurricane Katrina, Kimball volunteered to lead the Louisiana Supreme Court's effort to rebuild the state's court system. She was working in her office in the Baton Rouge courthouse, but "there was twelve feet of water in the New Orleans' Supreme Court courthouse," she says. "Judges got out of there floating on pieces of furniture. In Baton Rouge, I came in every morning at 6:00 AM to set up court, so I could assist in getting lawyers for the prisoners. That was a time. It was unbelievable." Kimball says she worked eighty to one hundred hours a week, a workload that she says may have induced the stroke she suffered while she was at it. Seven years later in 2012, Kimball was still working on problems arising from Hurricane Katrina when she announced her retirement.

Kimball completed her undergraduate studies in three years. She had two children while she was in law school. She opened her own practice in her twenties. She was first elected to a judgeship in her thirties. She was the first woman member of the Louisiana Supreme Court. And she became its chief justice in 2009.

Kimball, clearly a premium brand, says, "It would not occur to me to want to do something and fail." She continues, "Have a sense of fairness," and says it helps if you demand it from everyone in return.

But it's not enough on Election Day to be a superachiever, or fair and hardworking and caring. Those qualities make you a premium brand, but if you don't win on Election Day, where did they get you? This is where grit and, if necessary, being willing to go straight to the top to get what you want, come in.

During her 1992 campaign for a seat on the Louisiana Supreme Court, Kimball thought campaign funds raised by the Clinton for President campaign were not being distributed equitably in Louisiana. She says she didn't want a disproportionate share, but she did want a fair share. She called and made her case to John Breaux, Louisiana's senior US senator at the time, who made her case to the Clinton presidential campaign. The allocation changed. She got her fair share.

Premium branding means you can't avoid tough fights or tough issues. Otherwise, what's the value of your brand? The consequence is that, like Tylenol, premium brand people have an occasional bad run. For instance, after Justice Kimball announced her retirement in the spring of 2012, there was a dispute over who should succeed her. While the justices deliberated, Justice Bernette Johnson took them, including Kimball, to federal court, alleging race discrimination. The district court judge ruled on behalf of Johnson, positioning the first African American woman to sit on the Louisiana Supreme Court to become the state's first African American chief justice. Subsequently the supreme court justices met and issued a unanimous ruling stating that Johnson's "years of appointed and elected service on the high court give her the seniority" to be Kimball's successor. No doubt, there was heartache in the process and hard feelings developed. The Louisiana court system and Justice Kimball took some hits in the press. None of us can know what these two supremely gifted women, who both fought hard and used their connections to make their case to get ahead, talked about as Justice Johnson took over. They made history in the process: This transition in state supreme court chief justices is the first in American history in which a woman of color has succeeded a white woman. Any woman succeeding another woman in this job has only happened three times previously and all since 2001.

Consider this a cautionary tale, but don't let it dissuade you from developing your standout brand.

Strategic imperatives for building a premium brand:

★ Deliver what's expected on time and on budget.

★ Based on this proof of your right to be a premium brand, identify words that characterize your approach to your work.

★ Live up to those descriptors every day.

★ When difficult moments arise, don't let those difficulties bring down the value of your brand by diverting your attention from the words that accurately describe you.

★ Use that commitment to stay focused on your agenda and what others expect from you.

PART II

TAKE ON THE BIG BOYS

11

The only limitations on you
are the ones you impose

As you launch your campaign, there will probably be people who will call you names. You may be called a "ball-breaker" and other ugly names, like "bitch." If you're the sort of person who follows politics, this probably won't surprise you. But that sort of immaturity isn't the kind of thing that will derail a go-getter like you. Name calling is a sign of weakness. Caving to it demonstrates fear. The worst mistake you can make is allowing yourself to be limited by fear.

Julia Stasch says, "I always wanted to play on a big stage." And for her, she says, "The notion of boundaries is incompatible with the notion of power. The more your limit yourself, the less you can achieve." At the same time, Stasch is "always about setting the table so more people can participate," according to her colleague and friend Lori Healey. What an unbeatable combo.

Stasch knows whereof she speaks: her high-level jobs have included running a real estate development company, a bank, and a municipal department. Stasch preceded Healey as chief of staff to Chicago Mayor Richard M. Daley. Before that, she was deputy director of the General Services Administration, which constructs federal buildings. Now she is vice president for US programs at the John D. and Catherine T. MacArthur Foundation, giving away hundreds of millions of dollars annually to public programs throughout the country.

Stasch's career has consisted of running big enterprises for powerful men. After all, men own or are in charge of most of the big enterprises. What this means is that she's at the top of her game. Her demeanor is no fuss, no muss; steady and calm. But there's nothing steady or calm about her work. She knows a lot about a lot, and if she has to learn a new subject in order to address it successfully, she does.

I have worked with Stasch for more than three decades on a variety of complex projects covering health, housing, and employment issues and engaging numerous institutional partners. When we launched a campaign to increase the availability of the French "abortion pill" RU-486 in the United States, Stasch hadn't had any previous experience with reproductive rights advocacy, but she dug in hard. She called on her own resources, learned the material cold, and became an extremely effective spokesperson for the project.

In 2012, the *Chicago Tribune* said the following about her: "A behind-the-scenes visionary and politically savvy strategist, she has an ability to distill complex research and cut to the chase that has served her well as she endeavors to help change the face of business, civic and everyday life in Chicago and the nation."

Getting there hasn't come without sacrifices. Stasch says that if your goal is significant power in and at the top of male-run institutions, you can toss the notion of work-life balance right out the window. "I always felt that, if you're doing something important, your job is a lifestyle job. It's worth pouring yourself into it if you want it to be a path to power and influence. You have to put yourself behind it. You have to be willing to think about the job all the time because I don't understand how it can get done right otherwise."

Of course, this philosophy isn't for everyone. But we're not talking about everyone. We're talking about you, the woman who wants her political power to have no limits.

Stasch points out that a lot of what you can do for others is "locked up in your head," while you're in the office addressing immediate needs.

The office just doesn't offer the quiet time needed for creative problem solving. Stasch turns this hard truth into a positive, too: "Never being turned off enables me to see connections and ideas that serve me well." This means that each Sunday, she spreads her work papers and notes from the week out on the living room floor to see what to make of them in the coming week.

According to Stasch, it's a waste of time worrying about what you don't know. You need to be as prepared as you can be and then "go through the door"—or you'll never realize the opportunities on the other side. Instead of limiting herself by worrying that she may not know everything, Stasch says, she thinks about what she can do to help, how she can use her job to leverage a social good, how she can shepherd resources in the right direction. How she can focus the job and get things done.

When Stasch and I first got together on behalf of the women's center I cofounded, one of our programs trained women interested in the construction trades. At the time, Stasch was an executive in a large downtown commercial-real-estate development firm. She says, "I cared about racial justice and gender equity. I wanted to use my job to do something [to those ends]." She and the executive director and I talked. How could we create roles in their construction projects, including large downtown projects, for the center's clients? Stasch says, "I realized I could turn construction projects into income building and wealth building."

Stasch put the idea of placing women in construction jobs into action on a public-works project where the commitment would draw a lot of attention. The program she created for the company was more substantial than it might otherwise have been. Stasch had not permitted any false limitations to restrict her thinking and doing. As a result of letting her imagination exceed the imagined limitations of the project, she achieved her own greater power.

The distance between a good idea and making it real is shorter when a leader gets behind it. "I always want to lead," says Stasch. This might seem like a problem if you want to be powerful within male-dominated institutions, including governments. But to Stasch it's not, and it need not be to you, either. Consider this advice from Stasch:

"Powerful men have so much to do. There is so much to get done that it's always possible to carve out something you can lead." When she did this, she says, "He [the man in charge] didn't have to say do it. He just had to say don't not do it, which of course I rarely heard. I took advantage of reflected influence."

Stasch and I talked about how being the sort of person who doesn't buy into limitations requires certain qualities in a woman. They include strengths that men may view negatively. They include being blunt. We talked about worrying about "being nice" and how the effort to "be nice" can create a barrier to getting a job done, which can get in the way of your own ability to do it well. But as Stasch points out about her former boss, "Most of all, a mayor needs someone to get things done." In other words, if you pursue political power and responsibility at a high level, execute well. That will more than make up for any perceived personality flaws.

If being blunt and efficient means being called a bitch, so what? If you're running the show for the big boys—or better yet, taking them on—bitch it is.

When Bill Clinton was elected president in 1992, he invited Stasch to be the deputy director of the federal General Services Administration. Stasch proved herself supervising the construction of a new Oklahoma City federal building after the original was destroyed in the 1995 bombing. Clearly, she got big things done with dispatch, setting no limits on her own ability to work hard for her boss's benefit. Mayor Daley needed a building commissioner, so he turned to her, eventually making her chief of staff. When the MacArthur Foundation needed a head of US grant making, it turned to Stasch as well. She had shown repeatedly that she knew how to handle delicate political situations and keep everyone at the table.

Each of these powerful positions built her power and led to the next. In the process of doing each of these jobs, she developed that "reflected influence," which positioned her to be chosen for another powerful role. That will happen to you, too, if you follow her example.

It won't be easy, of course. Not having limits is intimidating because it requires full-throttle effort. But if you say I'm willing to do this but not that, or work today but not tomorrow, or deal with these people but not those, you'll deny yourself that no-boundaries power.

For some it's a trade-off, but apparently not for Stasch. "I love to think about my work," she says. If you do, too, then don't create unnecessary boundaries—there will be plenty of real ones.

Stasch does "have a life," as we unfortunately often put it—as if working isn't a vital part of living, when for so many of us it is. She's married, and though she and her husband don't have children, he takes care of things on the home front. From a practical standpoint, this arrangement is very helpful. But regardless of your own support system, it's important not to let your marital, partnership, or family status preclude you from living the no-limits job and reaping the political power that comes with it.

Some political women have partners or spouses who have to make choices similar to theirs, so lifestyle adaptations are understood as a matter of course. But that's not necessarily the norm, so it's best to make your desires known early on in a marriage or a partnership. Or, as my friend Melody Spann-Cooper puts it, "Cut your deal on the front end." Spann-Cooper runs Midway Broadcasting, which owns the historic black radio station WVON. She has a lot of family responsibilities as well as a demanding job, and she says that a powerful woman should be sure to tell her partner at the outset of the relationship what her political plan is. She can also say, "I'm willing to take turns, and you can even go first, but I must have my shot. I won't be prevented from pursuing my dream by what I agreed to help you accomplish. I need and deserve mine, too."

Strategic imperatives for building a no-limits approach:

★ Seek out and serve men who have big agendas and significant influence or power that they may be willing to share.

★ Identify the power of theirs you can make a case for sharing.

★ Make that case.

★ View your career as a calling, not as a job.

12

Dive in and start swimming

Too many women who want to seek and hold public office are afraid to dive in. Some think merely jumping in is corrupting. Others think you have to be an insider to win. Some will only enter with an invitation, after someone else decides they've earned it.

But when you jump in the political pool on your own and assert your right to be there, whether you're fighting a righteous cause or because you want to be a political somebody, don't assume the competition will be fair. To choose another metaphor, take the hits, go back to your corner, wipe the sweat off your brow, and come back swinging.

Of course, the bigger the contest, the bigger you look. It's counterintuitive, but when you volunteer to swim with the big fish, rather than coming off as small fry, you announce yourself as a big fish, too.

When you set your sights on Election Day, this perception of being a big fish yourself will allow you to swim in the pond with other, better-known contenders. Don't let modesty get in the way of your ambitions. You may step up and speak up because you deserve the position you want and you know you'll do a good job.

Barack Obama is an excellent role model in this department: two years in the Senate, no foreign policy experience, and no executive experience, yet he presumed to believe that he could be president of the United States. He didn't let his short resumé deter him, nor was he deterred by the fear that others would accuse him of hubris. He simply stated he wanted the job and was willing to enter the ring to fight for it. He knew that undertaking big battles would render him actually important, positioning him for the big win. Soon enough, that short resumé was forgotten, and people were more interested in watching how he did in the fights. And we all know how that turned out. He held his own. He looked and acted like an equal. He knew as much about the issues as his opposition. No one doubted his viability. He won. And won again.

Sarah Palin is another person who didn't let modest qualifications deter her: small-town mayor, governor of a state with very few people, no federal experience, but, apparently, no compunctions about running for vice president. Modesty was not going to be useful to her either. She knew that the sooner she dove in with the big boys, the sooner her big Election Day would be at hand.

You don't have to like these folks or agree with their political views to appreciate their strategic brilliance: they knew that picking a fight with the big guy could help in the effort to beat him. Louisiana governor Huey Long, my favorite example of this truism, knew it too. Before he was governor, Long was twenty-five and running as an unknown for a seat on the Louisiana Public Service Commission. But he didn't spend his time writing position papers or trying to get the big boys to like him: he picked a fight about rate increases with Standard Oil, the biggest boy in Louisiana at the time. He said this huge company was his enemy, criticizing it vociferously and constantly making speeches to people struggling to pay their utility bills. Because he was its singular opposition, Huey Long became its equal.

The path all three of these candidates took to the big ring was the same: declare your big ambition unabashedly, directly take on the biggest opposition to your achieving it, stand in the ring, and duke it out.

Debbie Stabenow is one of only thirty women ever elected to the US Senate, and she's been reelected twice. Stabenow was in her mid-twenties when she first ran for office in Michigan, beating an older and more established candidate. Before that, she managed her husband's campaign for election to the county board of commissioners. When he lost, he said to her, "You should run. You're the one who likes campaigning and talking to people." She is still proud of that first race: "Every other house had a yard sign."

Stabenow's opponent was an incumbent with deeper roots in the community. He had more political experience, but Stabenow ignored his advantages and moved ahead with belief in herself and her cause: keeping the local nursing home open to low-income senior citizens in the county who depended on it.

Stabenow did not know the minutiae of health-care policy, nor did she know all the ins and outs of nursing home operations. But she knew if she won, nursing home residents could use Medicaid to pay their bills. Her opponent led the effort to close the nursing home. During the campaign, he referred to Stabenow as "that young broad."

Stabenow knew she was young. But she knew she could and would learn more. "All of your experiences are valuable in public service," Stabenow says. "You don't need a political science degree."

Bottom line: She knew that kicking those poor seniors out of the nursing home was wrong. Hers was a righteous cause, and that was enough. Her place was on the Board of Commissioners if she was to do anything about it. Time to get in the ring, she thought. However, she waited to be asked. She's glad her husband encouraged her, but she also says about waiting, "Don't." (Planned Parenthood's Cecile Richards also said, "Don't wait to be asked. You won't be.") That's the last time Stabenow waited to be asked. She beat incumbents to become a state representative and US congresswoman, and in 2000 became the first woman to beat a sitting US senator in a general election.

And don't wait for a mentor, either. He or she may not come along. Stabenow says, "Older male politicians at the time were pretty threatened by a young woman." They still are. The sooner you beat them, the sooner they will respect you. You'll be mentoring them.

Once Stabenow became a county commissioner, her opportunity to rise came up with the opportunity to be chair two years later. "I was interested in seeing the board change. It came to me as I went along that there were enough people here who would vote for me. The opportunity was there and I took it. Have enough confidence in yourself, if the opportunity presents itself; be willing to take the risk."

Stabenow grew up in a working family in a small town in northern Michigan. She says her parents were supportive of whatever she did and had high expectations for her, and her father never suggested she limit where she set her sights simply because she was a girl.

Lots of American girls grow up in this kind of family. But not every American girl, no matter how supportive her father is, wants to be a big political girl. If you do, and you also recognize that no matter how smart you are or how hard you work or how supportive your parents are, the odds of getting to the top are slim, there is great value in learning the Stabenow way of getting ahead of the competition: get in early, and take them on where they live.

The alternative is that your (likely male) opponent is inside the ring, on a platform above your head. He's in a circumscribed area where the action is, an insider, while you're outside climbing slippery, sweat-soaked ropes, just trying to get in the ring. Being different and being an outsider has its merits, as does distinguishing yourself as a caring person. At the same time, people fear outsiders, regardless of how good their ideas are, just because they are different. So once you've decided to campaign for public office, you need to work from the inside.

When you meet Senator Stabenow, you're struck by the modesty of her appearance, her pleasant personality, and her all-around niceness. When you meet Barack Obama, you feel the same way. Neither has that over-the-top bluster we associate with the concept of "taking on the big boys." But nice people are tough, too, and, yes, even immodest—immodest in their ambition to be somebody in order to benefit others. So, if you don't have the outsized personality you associate with winning candidates, no problem. Have outsized ambition. Understand that to realize that outsized ambition, you have to fight the big boys on their own turf to acquire the power to do things for the rest of us.

Strategic imperatives once you dive in:

★ Be clear on your agenda and its righteousness.

★ Be willing to declare its righteousness to anyone who will listen.

★ Be willing to buttonhole anyone who resists.

★ Learn as soon as you can the mechanics of winning small elections—they'll make the case for your right to win bigger ones.

★ Don't wait until you know every policy nuance to make the decision to run. Your competition will be winning by then.

★ Don't ever wait to be asked to run.

13

Men are your enemies
(except when they're your friends)

There are three reasons men are your enemies. (1) Only one of you can win. (2) Too many of them still consider it inappropriate for women to be aggressive. You can't win without being aggressive, so where does that leave you? Exactly nowhere. (3) Many men haven't figured out yet that causes of particular concern to women affect all of society.

Men are your enemies, until they're your friends. Or as a friend of mine says, men are your competition, until they're not. You'll read here that if you fight as hard as you can to win, your (usually male) opposition will realize after you win that he wants to be your friend.

Walking down Last Chance Gulch, the main street of Helena, Montana, you won't see any hard-up miners, but you will see an old-time candy store, coffee shops, outdoor gear stores, and a couple of pottery galleries. Helena is home to the world-famous Archie Bray Foundation, a ceramic-arts center, where I serve on the board of directors. But Helena isn't an artsy resort town full of one percenters and designer-clothing boutiques. It's the state capitol of a conservative western state, which happens to have an old brickyard where some potters figured out they could make pottery for cheap.

In Helena I'd heard a lot about Aidan Myhre before I met her, in 2010. I was told about her family's long and distinguished history in Montana politics and philanthropy. I was told that by the time Myhre was in her thirties, she was already a highly regarded public person. The Archie Bray board wanted to recruit her, and everyone seemed to agree that she was a perfect candidate. It was only after Myhre joined the board, however, that I learned of her heroic battle while serving on the Helena school board.

Myhre is elegant but not intimidating. She is friendly and always polite. You can't imagine her ever raising her voice. She is a young mother with a busy career, yet she finds lots of time to be active in her community.

Her reasons for getting involved as a political activist, she says, began with her concerns over economic inequality. "My big issue is the erosion of the middle class," she says. And she took note of how the problem was being compounded "in the school setting, where the achievement gap is increasing. I ran for the school board because of this concern. This small nugget is part of a bigger picture." Now that she's in office, she says, "This is the overriding umbrella for me in making decisions."

When the Helena school board proposed a health curriculum with a chapter on human sexuality for kindergartners, community members protested. The board went back to the drawing board, but its new proposal, issued in June 2010, during Myhre's first term, led to an outcry. The board went back to the drawing board again and ultimately adopted a curriculum including a sex education component beginning in the sixth grade. In her first term on the school board, Myhre led the board's successful effort.

"Women have a lot more at stake in the sexual arena than men do," she says. "We need to help young women make good choices for their future. Sex education is hugely important in helping them make those choices."

Some battles are peculiarly ours, girlfriends. And when those battles take place in conservative, rural communities like Helena, there can be hell to pay. In Last Chance Gulch it was a metaphorical shootout between the forces of common sense, led by Myhre, and her male-led opposition, who seemed determined to keep women ignorant, barefoot, and pregnant.

Myhre told me what happened: "If a [protestor] had brought out a gun, I wouldn't have been surprised. It was stunning to me the fear tactics they used: blowing things out of proportion, claiming I wanted to teach kindergartners about blow jobs; people came from all over the country." Myhre says the people who testified in opposition to the adoption of the curriculum "had no respect for what young women are going through, for the school and social pressures they face. That was scary to me."

"Sweet, stay-at-home moms were put up as candidates [for the school board] to run against us. It was an amazing process." Myhre says she felt "the men who opposed it, at bottom, wanted to control their families."

Myhre had a bit of an epiphany. "When I woke up to the reality that the opposition wouldn't change their minds, that they would oppose no matter what, I felt completely comfortable with my decision and my vote." But she had to figure out how to prevail once the matter came up for a vote. She started working on a compromise.

"My personality is a little bit of a mediator," she says. "It was very easy for me to say then, 'OK, this is a really easy decision.' The original proposal was to start the curriculum in kindergarten. Let's address it starting in sixth grade, instead. We vetted it. We thought about it." She says, "[When we were finished] there was no hesitation or remorse. There were strong feelings, but the vote was done." The curriculum with the compromise language passed.

In the process of developing this compromise, men who had been Myhre's enemies became her friends. They did so because she had stood her ground on an important issue and had won. In 2011 Myhre won her campaign for reelection to the school board and was subsequently elected vice chair.

Myhre had room to make a compromise and still win a significant victory. But that's not always going to be the case. On Election Day only one person can win. And even in an advocacy campaign there isn't always room for compromise.

Years before Myhre's battle over the Helena schools' sex education curriculum, in the late 1970s, I led a campaign by the Illinois Women's Agenda, a coalition of women's organizations, to convince Illinois's new governor, James R. "Big Jim" Thompson, to appoint a "women's advocate." We had argued throughout the prior campaign year that the governor should be accountable to all Illinois women, directly and personally, not via some low-level person hidden in the bowels of the downstate bureaucracy. The advocate's job would be to make sure that policies such as sex education which would directly benefit women would be adopted. Thompson the candidate promised to make the appointment. But Thompson the governor stonewalled.

We went to the media.

Here's a sampling of the headlines we generated during the campaign: "Women scorch Thompson." "Women's advocate: 'What's taking Thompson so long?'" "Too busy for women?" "Is Big Jim skirting women's issues?" "Big Jim's big jam: women not satisfied."

These are the kind of headlines you dream of when your opposition is unyielding, and sure enough, Thompson gave in. Even then, though, I didn't let up. I was quoted in the *Chicago Sun-Times* saying I was glad he had ended "months of indecision." I wasn't going to let him off easy, and I wanted him to know we'd still be watching to see that he followed through. I went on to say, "I can't help but think . . . that the only reason [the appointment] happened at all is because we kept pressuring him for a year on it." He made himself our enemy, so we fought him and won.

Once we won, though, the governor and I got on just fine. Sure as shootin' in Last Chance Gulch, Big Jim Thompson was my enemy until he was my friend. It wasn't personal when he fought us. We had won, exercising power our former enemy wanted access to.

Sharon Weston Broome, Louisiana state senator and president pro tempore of the Louisiana State Senate, says, "I think men let things roll off their backs more easily than women do." When Governor Thompson acceded to our demand, he said, Come visit me. Let's talk. Let's be friends.

When people say "It's nothing personal," they're expressing a truth about politics that you need to get your head around, too: you're fighting as hard as you can for a cause you believe in that will benefit everyone. You're fighting for a better world, not for yourself. Your enemies are the enemies of your cause, not of you.

Why shouldn't the men you defeat partner with you? You were right. Why shouldn't you welcome them as friends? You should. Think again about Myhre's main reason for fighting for sex ed. She was fighting to create opportunities for young women to succeed, by giving them the education they need to make healthy personal choices. Men can help. Welcome them to your side.

Another lesson from my experience is that being polite is not the same thing as being nice. Being nice won't convince your opposition to back down. For Myhre on sex ed and for me with the women's advocate, the battle was won because we were unyielding in our commitment to achieve a larger good. "Unyielding" isn't usually too "nice." So be it.

Strategic imperatives for winning friends and influencing men:

★ Take on the biggest opponent you can: he's the guy who can help you the most after you beat him.

★ The bigger the race and the bigger the issues you address, the smaller the opposition will appear.

★ Figure out what qualities of yours make that opponent admire you. Then accentuate them as you campaign.

★ Guilt-trip your opposition. How can you, you big boy, not be for better schools? (Or for whatever is your signature campaign issue.)

★ But eliminate any tactics that might hurt you after the election—regardless of whether you win or lose. Either way, you want to survive to run again.

★ Make sure your message about why you should win is as expansively drawn as possible. That's the kind of message that will make your opposition feel like it must join you after Election Day.

★ And always remember what the big boys never, ever forget: Nice won't endear you to your enemies. But winning will.

14

Be willing to take an unyielding stand when your principles demand it

The duty of policy advocates, legislators, and other public officials is to get something useful done, which often involves compromise and negotiation. The ability to work with the opposition will also increase your effectiveness and value as a public servant and admired leader. However, compromise and negotiation don't work if your principles aren't firm. That's because it is your duty to lead with the strength of your convictions and your willingness to manage the effects of acting on them. Otherwise, why bother?

In 2006 Cecile Richards became president of the Planned Parenthood Federation of America, whose mission is promoting every woman's right to "manage her fertility." During her stewardship, the organization, which supports a woman's right to choose between abortion and carrying a fetus to term, has faced enormous challenges to its funding model—even to its continued existence. In 2012 Susan G. Komen for the Cure decided to pull its support of Planned Parenthood, and the House of Representatives voted to defund it. As Richards told the *Daily Beast*, "Providing basic birth control and cancer screening and well-woman checkups for women that are uninsured is not something that the health-care system in America is eager to do. That's why

Planned Parenthood provides services to three million patients every year." In an interview with the *Washington Post*, she described being under siege: "It was the first time, really, we'd ever seen Congress go after Planned Parenthood as an organization—not just being against choice or other issues—and to make a foursquare effort to get rid of the entire family-planning program in the United States, and to have such a big vote on it in the US House was historic. They named us by name, and women really identified with this. It wasn't just, well, times are tough, we're going to cut family planning services, it was literally we're going to tell women they can't go to the major family-planning provider in this country."

My friend Ellen Chesler, biographer of Planned Parenthood founder Margaret Sanger, describes Richards as "a transformational leader." Chesler is describing a woman who has made Planned Parenthood into one of the most successful political organizations in the United States, able to engage millions at a moment's notice to advocate for its cause and to engage public officials, from the president on down, on a moment's notice, too.

"She was above the fold on the front page of the *New York Times* two days in a row [talking about reproductive health]," says Chesler. "I didn't think I'd ever live to see that happen." Planned Parenthood's directors were traditionally health-care professionals, not expert politicians. Transformational leaders don't always rise from the expected places.

Richards began her professional life organizing hospital and hotel workers, and after serving as deputy chief of staff for California congresswoman Nancy Pelosi, she went on to found a national coalition of grassroots Democratic organizations. "I only lasted on Capitol Hill a year and a half," says Richards. "There are people who love that life. It was not good for me: I'm an advocate."

Time magazine's 2012 list of the one hundred people it deems "most influential" says that Richards "is a role model for all of us as she leads women in pursuit of unfettered access to health care and reproductive freedom." Richards herself says, "Women—we always think we have to make a 'one hundred' on everything. We have a million messages we send ourselves."

The choice of which messages to pay attention to is ours.

During the debate over whether there would be abortion coverage in the Affordable Care Act, which mandates health-care coverage for every American and passed in 2010, Planned Parenthood had to make a hard decision, not design a compromise. They ended up taking a stand insisting on coverage for abortions. Richards says, "This was a moment in our history in which we had to decide what line we won't cross. If we weren't going to stand up for women's reproductive rights, who would?"

Christine C. Quinn, elected speaker of the New York City Council in 2006, does things the right way, too. Pearl River, New York, the New York City suburb where I grew up, was founded by a German immigrant and settled by lots of Lutherans. But by the time we were living there, New York City police officers and fire fighters had moved in, and it seemed everyone in politics and public office was Irish Catholic. Many childhood nights, I went to bed wishing I were Kathleen Mulcahy, my best friend across the street, because she was born into the Pearl River in-crowd. In Pearl River, Saint Patrick's Day is one of the holiest days of the year, with, of course, a parade at its center. Yet Quinn, an Irish American now governing millions of Irish Catholic New Yorkers, has had the courage to boycott the New York City Saint Patrick's Day parade because of the anti-gay position of its sponsoring organization, the Ancient Order of Hibernians, and of New York's powerful Irish Catholic cardinal, Timothy Dolan, even as she collaborated with him on other public matters, such as poverty and immigration.

The phrase "The personal is political" gained currency in the late 1960s among feminists seeking to show that all relationships involve power and have political ramifications and that almost all personal acts have political meaning. I still see it all the time, including once not long ago on a screen crawl on TV during a discussion of "black hair," and it still serves as a reminder that big or small, personal acts—say, how you wear your hair—reveal who you are politically. When you acknowledge that the personal is political, making your personal choices and advocacy congruent with your public life signals who you are loud and clear.

Cecile Richards is the daughter of the late Texas governor Ann Richards, remembered for her white bouffant hair, sharp tongue, and sharper wit. Ann Richards's *New York Times* obituary led with her famous joke about the vice president, George H. W. Bush, in her keynote speech at the 1988 Democratic National Convention: "Poor George, he can't help it—he was born with a silver foot in his mouth." Another *New York Times* article says Ann Richards was "a real pistol who drawled truth to power, stripping politics of pretense."

At the governor's daughter's New York office, in an otherwise standard-issue corporate conference room, hangs a photo showing Mom with her Harley-Davidson. Clearly Cecile Richards is using the photo as shorthand for a message she wants to send all her visitors: Cecile Richards is proud of her mother the ass kicker, so chances are she's an ass kicker, too.

Strategic imperatives for standing your ground:

★ Keep in mind at all times the policy lines you won't ever cross.

★ Once you've made this list, share it with your family, close friends, and key supporters, so that there is no ambiguity in their minds regarding how you will proceed at certain turning points.

★ Also advise your colleagues and coworkers of what those lines are, so they don't get confused in their daily work or make errors in judgment that become difficult for you to manage, or worse, try to explain away.

★ Develop and have at the ready your organizing strategies and public messages for responding to pressure to change your mind.

★ Don't be timid about using those strategies. Remember that people of goodwill can and do disagree. That's your right.

15

Lead with your strength, even if it's perceived negatively by some

You have to go with your strength to win, even if your strength is generally perceived as a negative quality. The times demand it. Victory for your cause demands it. Consolidating your power demands it. Doing the right thing for women who don't have the voice and power you have demands it. If you doubt what I'm telling you, think Cleopatra or Catherine the Great or Indira Gandhi, warrior queens all.

Here is a tale out of school—high school, that is. It's the story of the high school senior voted Most Likely to Succeed but also Most Argumentative. What's a girl to do? Especially one with big plans for her future that depend on her willingness to speak up and out. Well, the answer, as I learned decades later, is to forge ahead, realizing that the attributes that make you willing and able to do the work required to succeed (such as argumentativeness) may be attributes the public will appreciate most of the time and forgive when needed.

In the fall of 2012, news reports following the tragic bombing of the US consulate in Benghazi, Libya stated that the late ambassador had made a request for additional security that the State Department denied. That revelation was damning enough. Then President Obama's adviser David Axelrod said, "These were judgments that were made by security folks at the State Department," after Vice President Joe Biden said this matter had never reached his or the president's desk.

Two days later, in Lima, Peru, where she was a long way from home and from pestering reporters, secretary of state Hillary Clinton put an end to the finger pointing. "I take responsibility," Clinton told CNN. "I'm in charge of the State Department's sixty-thousand-plus people all over the world." Where was the upside for a woman who may well want to run for president in claiming responsibility for what some called an error in judgment that cost American lives?

There are a couple: She demonstrates loyalty to her boss, as well as the confidence that she can fall on her sword now but rise again to a position of strength. Days later, when President Obama made the counterargument taking responsibility himself for all matters involving foreign affairs, Clinton looked good for having tried.

Frank Bruni, writing about the 2012 presidential debates in the *New York Times*, said it best in an op-ed titled "Never Waver, Never Wobble": "What fools most of us are. What chumps. We worry about our flaws, sweat our mistakes, allow the truth to be our tether and let conscience trip us up. We tiptoe. We equivocate. The political arena would make mincemeat of us."

Is your optimism your strength? I think issue advocates are frequently glass-half-full types. Especially those who are the first to advocate a position that demands real systemic change or reveals harsh and unpleasant truths in the process. If this sounds like you, you're probably one of those "Most Argumentative" types, too. And if you're now contemplating seeking office, don't try to hide this quality. You won't succeed. Instead, make the best of it. Here is how: I've counseled clients (as well as myself, when I needed a harsh reminder) to say, "I speak frankly because I care so much. I would be remiss on behalf of my organization, or constituents and others who suffer just like them, if I weren't." This approach turns being argumentative into a positive. How can anyone be against feeding hungry children, housing homeless people, or making sure girls get just as many college scholarships as boys do? They can't. Your perceived weakness, never being willing to back down to avoid a fight, is a virtue: you're willing to speak up for those who can't speak for themselves.

When Shirley Chisholm became the first African American woman to win a seat in Congress in 1968, she beat a man who had been the leader of a major civil rights organization. Four years later when she ran for president, she knew she couldn't win, but she did it to make a point: that women have a right and responsibility to run for president, too. She said she ran "in spite of hopeless odds . . . to demonstrate the sheer will and refusal to accept the status quo."

Chisholm's virtue is that to make a point she was willing to fight despite the odds, never saying never. Her strong and argumentative voice and direct style made her a trailblazer, not a loser.

Think about how your own qualities can be used to achieve a positive substantive victory for others. Perhaps, as Chisholm did, you win by simply getting your message across. Come Democratic Party convention time, Hubert Humphrey, the nominee who went on to lose to Richard Nixon, released all his African American delegates to Chisholm in a symbolic but potent gesture. When Chisholm returned to Congress, she was elected secretary of the House Democratic Caucus. And she only hired women to staff her congressional office.

Strategic imperatives for leading with your strength:

★ Inventory your strengths.

★ Characterize all of them positively.

★ Memorize the list, and repeat it forcefully whenever and wherever needed.

★ Lead projects that depend on your strengths for their success.

★ Notice that plenty of famous and successful men have qualities that could be characterized as either negative or positive. Point this out whenever you have the opportunity.

★ Consider the good those men could do because they possessed those qualities, and know you will do the same.

16

Find rich and powerful people and get them to do things for you

It seems counterintuitive, but rich and powerful people need validation, too. In the dark, predawn hours, even the biggest boys and girls wonder, Do I matter? Does anyone care? So when you ask for their support, including their money—it's a win-win: you get help, and they feel important. And if you win as a result of their help, they're validated and even more inclined to do nice things for you—sometimes without even being asked.

There are a lot of rich and, consequently, powerful people in politics. They are the donors; the pals of the officials whose favors they seek; the people who get invited to the exclusive parties, whether or not they've ever done anything substantive; the (mostly male) political consultants who earned enough to cash out, give speeches, and write books; the former elected officials who now make big bucks giving speeches to groups they professed to dislike while in office (any Democrat or Republican at a bankers' meeting); the middle-aged, usually male rich folks who decided that running for office would be fun; and the corporate titan political-action-committee funders.

The question for you isn't whether you will ask these folks for help with your campaign—the question is how to position yourself to make the ask. It's best to start this project as early as possible, because the sooner the rich and powerful become your friends, the sooner and better they can help you. As I've mentioned, the best place to start is as a fund-raiser, which puts you in the same rooms as the rich and powerful, where you can get to know them. As Planned Parenthood fund-raiser Laura Tucker put it, when you give your own time and money, "you end up in the same smaller rooms" as the women with lots of money.

My first professional job was as a $300-per-month staffer for the Chicago chapter of the American Jewish Committee (AJC), whose leadership is mostly well-off businesspeople, professionals, and philanthropists. I'd moved to Chicago three years earlier and spent my days in graduate school. Nothing in my Chicago experience so far had connected me to rich or powerful people.

The AJC fund-raising staff taught me how to find out who had money and power in Chicago and what they did with it. I learned to read the obituaries and gossip columns in the local newspapers and the *New York Times*. They taught me to commit to memory the boards of directors of local organizations, as well as the familial connections among those people. They also taught me how to identify and understand the interests of the women in this crowd, because my job was to engage them in AJC's work.

They also taught me to get to know and understand the webs of relationships around public officials who could help; be conversant about the favorite causes and interests of these influential Chicagoans; be willing to ask them for money; and characterize their financial gifts as investments, suggesting a broader (and more useful to AJC) role in undertaking the project the investment made possible.

I had recently read a book that reinforced the tactics behind this assignment. C. Wright Mills contends in *The Power Elite* that those in "political, economic, and military circles, which are an intricate set of overlapping small but dominant groups, share decisions having at least national consequences. Insofar as national events are decided, the power elite are those who decide them."

Because I already knew I wanted to be where decisions with "national consequences" were made, my path was clear: Get to know the members of Chicago's power elite. Get to know personally as many individual members as possible. Recruit as many as I could to my "candidacy"—in other words, the AJC cause, and then to my personal one, for whatever I decided I wanted to do.

I got to work. When I did, I learned an important lesson Laura Tucker, who started out as a staffer just like me, says she learned as well: "Rich people are people too. Don't be intimidated, and they will respect you. If you're talking to someone who has a strong sense of self, they're looking for someone who also has a strong sense of self. I want someone who is going to talk to me as a person."

Part of that "talk to me as a person [not as a checkbook]" strategy involves talking about issues of mutual concern. When I do this, common concerns frequently lead to common projects. When a group of friends and I started the women's center I mentioned before, to advocate for public policy benefiting women, AJC women leaders helped us launch the center. A couple hosted "important parties" for us. I learned this useful term from one of the women I met raising money for the National Women's Political Caucus. Say you're running for PTA president or for a seat on a local board. Your important parties will be the ones where you might have the opportunity to chat up the school superintendent, members of the board, the mayor, city council members, or leading businesspeople. All can help you make important things happen, including your election. Remember this mantra: it's not the menu or the venue; it's who will be eating and meeting.

At AJC, I also learned that it's useful to be the organizer of as many of these important parties as you can. You don't have to be important to take on this job. You volunteer to do the organizing because you want what that party will give you: a chance to meet powerful people who can help you. Each time, ask as many rich and powerful women to host as you can and makes sense. Then ask them to invite their friends, who will include other rich and powerful women. Then volunteer to personally invite each of those women to attend. You've now developed three interlocking circles of women who can help you.

As that important party's organizer, you're working with the hosts, but it's crucial to never forget that you're the staffer. You always want to be forthright and clear, but polite and deferential. You don't need to be obsequious, but you should be enthusiastic and organized without being overbearing. After all, courting wealth and power can backfire if you blow it.

While you're organizing, you will learn all about the "power elite" in your community, including each person's favorite cause. This will come in handy as you develop campaign strategies and policy positions: you'll learn their views and be able to take the measure of them, and this will enable you to fold these decision makers into your efforts.

If the organizing has a fund-raising component, remember another mantra: fund-raising is organizing. When you ask people for money, you have to make your case convincingly, which means knowing the substantive merits of the case, not only why it's rhetorically compelling or politically smart. This will also help you build out from one relationship to the next.

If you find this approach distasteful, take a lesson from the Nancy Pelosi playbook. The first woman Speaker of the US House of Representatives built her career by being a fund-raiser. When the local congressional seat opened up, she was right there, close to the seat of power, having been instrumental in the retiring member's elections.

During her career, Pelosi also learned about the issues facing her community, how her community worked, and how it made decisions. Of course, that is also how she raised all that money: she understood her community, including its rich and powerful.

Which brings me to my next piece of advice: You have to look like you belong in the important-party room. Do wear that black suit. Wear it as often as you need to. Fashion consultants say that people make judgments about one another within thirty seconds of meeting. Black suits work in thirty seconds. So do good, if modest, jewelry and shoes that emanate power. (Those would be the ones with heels.)

My first powerful woman mentor gave me this advice. In fact, her advice started with the bit about the shoes. She even told me where to buy good ones at a discount. (My mother had already taught me about the good, if modest, jewelry.)

A lot of guessing goes on about how much money people have. You're not the only one who knows where to find designer shoes at a discount. That woman you're getting to know, the one who always wears beautiful clothes and great jewelry and lives in that beautiful house, may have less than you think. Maybe she used to be in a position to buy those clothes or that house but isn't anymore. Maybe she comes from the same modest background as so many other powerful women do and has significant family responsibilities back home. Maybe some husband or boyfriend laid it all on her recently and could just as easily take it all away. Or maybe the company where she's a big-time executive is about to go under, or the CEO who hired her is about to get fired, and she knows that but you don't. (I'm floored by the number of powerful, wealthy women who have confided to me that they worry every day about being a bag lady one day! More to lose, I guess.)

Knowing these possibilities exist doesn't mean I don't ask (though it does mean I don't tell). And you will have to do the same. After all, you're only asking her to help other women get what she's got: sufficient means and power to do good for other women.

Here are some other truths about working successfully with the rich and powerful.

Grace, accomplishment, and selflessness are attributes that deserve special respect. Having money doesn't. See W. C. Fields: "A rich man is nothing but a poor man with money."

Because there is always somebody out there with more money or more power, rich and powerful people are constantly jockeying for position. Use that jockeying to your advantage.

A lot of rich people want to appear selfless because they know you know they didn't get rich being that way. Responding to your requests for help makes them feel good about themselves.

Rich and powerful people hang around with their own kind. This means their friends who can help you are very close at hand, and introductions are yours for the asking—if you ask the right way.

Strategic imperatives for getting to important parties and making the circuit work for you:

★ When you're organizing the party, keep inviting until you're sure the room will be full—after all, you're only calling because you care.

★ Claim a victory when you've filled the room. Even the fanciest people worry about giving a party and no one attending.

★ Whether you're a staffer, candidate, or guest, wear a jacket and keep a note in your pocket listing the names of people you want to meet.

★ Stand near the room's entrance, so that you can welcome people, even if you're not present in any official capacity.

★ If you're a guest, arrive when the most people are likely to be there. That's usually midway, right before the speeches will be starting.

★ Stand in the doorway and look around to see who's there.

★ If there are people you already know who you want to talk to, do that first.

★ Walk the room until you find the people on your list you don't know, and talk to them.

★ Just like there's no cleavage or drinking in the boardroom, there's no cleavage or drinking at an important business party. If you have time left over, have fun then.

★ Keep your wits about you at all times.

★ The line between making people feel generous and making them feel taken advantage of is a thin one. Figure out where it is by understanding what makes each individual you meet resistant or defensive, and don't cross it.

17

Use your connections to advance your cause (just like the men do)

When Lisa Madigan, now in her fourth term as Illinois attorney general, first ran for the position in 2002, she was accused of being an insider because her father, Michael Madigan, is the Speaker of the House in the Illinois General Assembly. Some say that in his hands the office has become the most powerful position in Illinois government. People who don't care for Speaker Madigan or his policies pooh-pooh the attorney general's accomplishments because of this family connection.

When you're an insider, many people presume that you're working on an agenda that's somehow different from the public's best interests. This belief is not without a historical basis, but it's also not always true. Lisa Madigan's connections were perceived as a negative by some, but she had the option of making them a positive. How can connections be a bad thing if you're using them to benefit the right causes?

Having a family member in public office should not be a deal breaker for the woman who seeks election. Clearly this capital can be used to the good. Of course, male political dynasties hardly cause a raised eyebrow when it comes to the qualifications of their members.

Yet I see too many women who want to seek public office fall prey to the fear that voters or appointing officials might find their political connections off-putting and decide not to put themselves forward. Others drive down another dead-end street—buying into the notion that women should somehow be purer than men and therefore shouldn't take advantage of being insiders.

How can you help, if you can't get into the position to be helpful because you've convinced yourself you don't deserve it?

I met Lisa Madigan when she was thinking about running for the Illinois state senate. A mutual friend introduced us, saying, "You'll like each other. You care about the same things." As we chatted, I learned that Madigan lived only a couple of Chicago alleys away. If she won, she'd be representing the legislative district next to mine.

Later, I mulled over our encounter. How did I feel about this young woman with no electoral experience starting her career in public office in the state senate? After all, most women don't get to start out that high up at so young an age. She could because she was the daughter of Mike Madigan. I was entertaining the usual prejudices against children of privilege.

As a practical matter, someone may open a door to a leadership opportunity, but the woman who walks through has to earn the votes. Floors all over the place are littered with supine guys who thought otherwise.

Madigan was knowledgeable and caring. Her resumé demonstrated that she had been engaged with public causes in meaningful ways. For instance, she had taught in South Africa and worked for a Chicago junior college in a neighborhood program fighting crime. Of course, I also knew she would know how to get elected. More women in public office benefits everyone, no matter who their daddies are. If the woman in that seat can call on powerful connections to benefit women, I'm down with that program.

When Madigan announced her state senate candidacy, our mutual friend, my husband, and I hosted a fund-raiser for her. And shortly thereafter, I noticed a lot of people knocking on doors in the neighborhood on her behalf. Madigan's campaign workers were out in force, and it's not unreasonable to assume that some were members of her father's formidable political organization.

However, Madigan says she met with every Chicago alderman and every Democratic committeeman with wards in the district she wanted to represent. Maybe she asked her father to make some introductions, but she made her own case, instead of assuming the support was hers by birthright. She also campaigned door-to door daily, visited schools and stores, and began the day shaking hands at train and bus stops. While meeting the district's voters, Madigan had a chance to demonstrate that being related to one of the state's most powerful politicians wasn't a disadvantage—it was an advantage for her, and it could also be for them. When Madigan won, the women of Illinois got another advocate in a state senate seat. Now Madigan is on short lists to be our first woman president, in part because she used her unique political capital to begin her career.

You should use every strength you've got to win the chance to govern, beginning and ending with your connections. Connections can supply donors and campaign workers. If they can help you become an expert on the issues, even better. Combine this access with your dialogue with the public, and you will win your Election Day.

And everyone has connections that matter. Maybe the connections to local business leaders you've developed running the local YWCA can help you run for school board. But you do have to ask them. If business colleagues can help you recruit campaign endorsers, ask. If teachers you know can help you become an expert on the issues, ask them. Combine your connections with your understanding of what you need to do to win, and you will win on Election Day.

Obviously, one of our most prominent national female figures, Hillary Clinton, had an advantage in politics thanks to her husband the president. But I wonder if anyone thinks about her impressive record as US secretary of state as a result of her marriage to the president. She took advantage of her connections and then transcended any criticism of that with her performance of her duties.

Catherine D. Kimball, chief justice of the Louisiana Supreme Court, was born into a political family with a web of powerful connections.

She married into another. She was first elected to a judgeship, the first-ever woman judge in her district, in 1992. When I went to see her, Kimball worked in a large courthouse you couldn't get inside without going through airport-type security. After you get past that, a big guy walks you to the elevator, rides up with you, and walks you down the hall to her office. That's where you found Justice Kimball behind a very big desk.

In her home parish, says Kimball, "Mother's father was the sheriff. After he died, his son, my uncle, became the sheriff." Her husband was a member of the Louisiana state house of representatives in the district where he grew up, and she first ran for judge replacing her husband's uncle, who was retiring. Kimball says her husband's being a politician was instrumental to her success. You get the picture. There are stories like this all over the country. Maybe, it's yours, too. No reason to back away from it. Kimball was a well-respected judge. Yet her Election Day victories were achieved in part by doing what insiders do, using their political network to position themselves for selection as the candidate, and then to run a campaign on their behalf.

Clearly, this kind of hardball isn't for the faint of heart or the woman who fears what political competition in the public square will always foster: criticism. But softball is only played at campaign photo-ops. Playing hardball is the way to win.

Winning women know that if you want to win on Election Day, you've got to make choices with your head on straight, and that means calling on your political connections to connect for you. Justice Kimball says, "Be who you are. The voting public knows when someone is a phony."

What voters want their public officials to be is problem solvers, not wishful thinkers who can't get votes. This is the virtue of being connected. You know what's going on, you are a part of it, and you can do something about it.

When Kimball decided she wanted to return to paid work after being a homemaker for a while, she "contacted the new federal district court judge and asked if I could clerk for him. I had gone to high school with the judge's children and knew the family all my life."

Strategic imperatives for developing and using your connections:

★ If you're not already an insider, become one by sharing your knowledge with insiders who may not have it and by steadily communicating with people who have connections you want, too.

★ Create a personal database that includes everyone you've ever met, regardless of whether or not you've interacted one-on-one.

★ Keep the database up to date in real time with contact information and details of each individual's interests (personal as well as policy), organizational affiliations, funding interests and commitments, media coverage, and current partner or marital status so that you make requests appropriately. Always include anything else that gives you a sense of the person, so that you're in context when you call to say you're ready to run.

★ Review the database at least quarterly, and write a note to those you haven't seen or talked with lately. Suggest getting together. Say you'd like to be a part of whatever they're doing.

★ If you've got your eye on something you want to run for, inventory the names in the database for their usefulness for this specific purpose. Then classify those people in four categories: (1) friends and colleagues who you keep close, would do anything for you, and are a midnight call away, if needed; (2) important people who those in group 1 can get you to; (3) people you haven't figured out a connection to but will, because you know you'll need them early on; and (4) those who can wait till later, but not too much later.

18

Don't worry if you're scared

Former New York City public advocate Betsy Gotbaum says, "Fear is your friend. The most courageous thing I've ever done is run for office."

Gotbaum is right. Your fear crystallizes thought and catalyzes action. It forces you to focus on the biggest challenges and tackle the hardest tasks. When you succeed, your fear will be one of the things that got you there. Your awareness of this will help you embrace your fear and avoid looking like a loser; you'll use it to your advantage.

That famous line from the Gillette campaign (pitched by onetime ad exec Donna Karan), "Never let them see you sweat," always jumps to mind when I'm fearful. At times like these, I also remember the wise counsel of a political girlfriend who reminds me to control what I can and forget the rest. When she's worried about a speech she has to give and how voters will react to it, she focuses on what to wear. Another mantra you can keep in mind is what Woody Allen said about success: 80 percent is just showing up.

When Rush Limbaugh called reproductive rights activist Sandra Fluke a slut in February 2012 after she testified to members of Congress about the need for an insurance mandate to cover birth control, Fluke, then a thirty-one-year-old law student, was deluged with the kind of attention generally reserved for Hollywood celebrities or politicians who've made really big mistakes. She became a devil to some and a hero to millions of others. Women (in particular) mobilized to demand that advertisers drop Limbaugh's radio show, and many did. Fluke was an unknown campus activist when she was invited to testify. She could not have anticipated either the vicious attack or the wave of approbation she received afterward.

If Fluke minded the scrutiny or was upset about being called names, she didn't blink an eye. She did acknowledge to the *Washington Post* that "there's been some highs and some lows." However, when President Obama asked her how she was doing, she said, "I'm OK." She told the *Washington Post*, "This reaction is so out of the bounds of acceptable discourse. . . . These types of words shouldn't be applied to anyone." She gave dozens of other interviews. She accepted speaking invitations. She became a hero, appearing on the cover of *Ms.* head-on, arms crossed, looking commanding, framed by the headline "You Called Me What? Sandra Fluke Stands Up for Our Bodies and Our Rights." She wrote about her experience for CNN, insisting "slurs won't silence women." She accepted invitations to be honored and to become a spokeswoman for political causes. She started a Twitter account that within days had tens of thousands of followers and a Tumblr account that was immediately filled with comments from fans. She was profiled in the *New York Times*. She publicly mulled over personal matters her newfound fame forced her to address.

Having shared the stage with President Obama and Cecile Richards at the 2012 Democratic National Convention, Fluke now has political influence and a bully pulpit grander than many who have spent a lifetime in politics. As evidenced by her actions, she rejected the alternative of running for cover. Doing so enabled her to achieve "feminist superstardom," according to the *New York Times*. She said to the *Los Angeles Times*, "I've always been an activist who's been speaking about these policies, it's just that more people are listening now. . . . But I'm trying to use the opportunity to make sure as many people as possible hear about these really important questions we're faced with right now."

When there's a pit in your stomach the size of the Grand Canyon because of what you're about to do, what you've already done, or what someone said about you, keep in mind that whatever it is can work for you on Election Day. Identify the opportunities the fearsome event can foster. Analyze them to find an immediate, positive opening for you. Develop a strategy to exploit that opening and exploit it right away.

As mayor of Camden, New Jersey, Dana Redd governs a city with one of the country's highest murder rates. She personally lives with murder every day. She became an orphan at age eight when both her parents were murdered in nearby Bordentown. Anyone in her place might have left town. But that's not what Redd did. As an adult, she faced her fear and became a cheerleader for the city, first as a state senator and city council member and then as mayor. Redd put it this way in a mayoral campaign press release: "I walk the streets of this city every day, and I know what our people are going through." I imagine you know what your people are going through, too: don't let fear deter you from helping them.

Fear can also be induced by self-doubt. When Deanna Archuleta, former senior adviser to Ken Salazar, President Obama's first-term secretary of the Department of the Interior, ran for office as a county commissioner in Bernalillo County, New Mexico, she tells me, a well-known member of Congress was in Santa Fe to campaign for a colleague. The congressperson told Archuleta there were only two ways to run for office: "Run opposed, or run scared." Archuleta says the notion of running scared "flipped up my stomach. I thought: 'What is this?' At that moment, I thought, I will never be scared. . . . If you are afraid, why are you doing it? Being afraid is no way to live a life. Every time I think I can't do something, those words come to mind. My personal philosophy is if you want something, you do what you need to do. You put the angst to work for you." Make the fear your helpful friend.

Kimberly Merchant, managing attorney of the Delta office of the Mississippi Center for Justice, puts her angst to work for her and her clients every day. She conquers a fear every political woman experiences: the fear of pushback because you are a strong woman seeking a political voice and platform.

Merchant grew up in modest circumstances on the Mississippi Gulf Coast and then moved to northern Mississippi to attend the University of Mississippi School of Law. She says she attended Ole Miss because she was offered a tuition waiver as the law school attempted to increase enrollment of black students. "It was my first taste of white privilege. A lot of these kids were driving their BMWs, living in condos—they already had everything. Their family members were attorneys and judges. When I got there, I didn't know any attorneys, much less judges." After graduation she moved to the Delta region, to Greenville (also home to Lisa B. Percy), another new place. But the Mississippi Delta isn't just any old place, as you've already gathered.

Retired Princeton University history professor Nell Irvin Painter describes the region in her *New York Times* book review of James C. Cobb's *The Most Southern Place on Earth: The Mississippi Delta and the Roots of Regional Identity*: "With a black majority that has long remained susceptible to all the ills that accompany abject poverty, the Mississippi Delta's quality of life usually comes in at the bottom. Meanwhile, the few at the pinnacle of Delta society are rich, leisured, and cultured. With no middle class to speak of, its masses oppressed, its rich rolling in dough, the Mississippi Delta may qualify as 'the most southern place on earth.'"

Merchant—young, single, and African American—moved there anyway. She went to work for Victor McTeer, a civil rights lawyer committed to remedying Delta injustice. After working for McTeer, Merchant was appointed assistant district attorney and ran for the office of justice court judge of Washington County.

Merchant was a well-qualified lawyer with roots in the community and married to a local police officer. But state law doesn't require the justice court judge to be a lawyer. Merchant lost the race by ninety votes. She says she lost because "it was not about qualifications." She also says she heard "Wait your turn" many times.

Merchant told me, "There were all these rumors about me. For example, that I was dating a guy who was a murderer whose case I tried! I never met him until I walked in the courtroom." Previously, "I was able to just 'do Kim' and not worry about what people said."

She puts it this way: "Of course, anytime you are taking on something new, there is fear involved. . . . I didn't know what I was going to do if I didn't win the justice job. A paycheck is very important." She regrouped. Merchant advises: face the fear, keep moving, and "be a positive, visible force for change." She also says, "I don't have a problem going against the grain. I don't let them kill my spirit. When you step out the door, you just have to keep moving."

Political women end up in many situations that can induce fear: speaking truths to the powerful on controversial topics, failing to adequately resolve distressing problems, confronting ghosts from the past, moving to strange places, facing criticism of job performance and personal life, and the anxiety that fighting back can create. But instead of responding to the fear in negative ways, you can acknowledge it, own it, and use it to your own advantage.

Strategic imperatives for dealing with fear:

- ★ Identify the causes of fear that can be addressed.

- ★ Address your worst fears directly in your campaign strategy.

- ★ Boost your own morale by finding the silver lining to your fears.

- ★ Be prepared to address the fear-inducing qualities of your opponent head-on and regularly—they are not going to go away.

- ★ Find those in the opposition who would like you if they knew you, and make them your friends.

- ★ Always talk like winning is just around the corner.

19

You'll need the big boys (who may be big girls) most of all; don't ever forget it

Bad news travels fast. Next to celebrity bad news, political bad news flies the fastest. Think of onetime presidential candidate John Edwards and his legal troubles and sordid personal life, or the repercussions of Susan G. Komen for the Cure targeting Planned Parenthood, or of Newt and Calista Gingrich and their Tiffany line of credit. I sure hope your bad news is never this big, but when it hits, your safely constructed network will save you.

Desirée Rogers came into her political career with solid training. Her father, Roy E. Glapion Jr., was a member of the New Orleans City Council, director of athletics for the New Orleans public school system, and president of the Zulu Social Aid and Pleasure Club, a predominantly African American Mardi Gras krewe that he built into a racially integrated and powerful civic organization. Glapion provided a good example to his children of how to navigate both the public and private sectors to good personal (as well as public) ends. Desirée Glapion married Chicagoan John Rogers, whose mother, Jewel Rogers Lafontant, was the first woman US deputy solicitor general, an ambassador, and influential figure in national Republican politics, introduced her to network building, influence building, and public service Chicago-style.

Judging by her accomplishments, Rogers learned these lessons well. She quickly became a civic, business, and political player in her adopted hometown. For example, early on, she directed the Illinois Lottery for a Republican governor, while her husband built his political career as a fund-raiser for Democratic candidates. Together, they built a wide circle of Democratic friends. Over time, that circle came to include Michelle and Barack Obama. When Barack Obama decided to run for the presidency, Desirée Rogers was the choice to host a Chicago fund-raiser for him at a critical juncture in the presidential campaign. When Obama won the presidency, Rogers was appointed White House social secretary, the first and only African American to ever hold the position. Breaking new political ground, Rogers moved her political power base to DC.

Well, you may recall how that chapter ended. Rogers was responsible for a state dinner that caused significant embarrassment for the Obama administration when security was breached by a DC couple. After they were caught, the couple made hay of their misadventure, posting photos of themselves at the dinner online. Even though the couple was not on the dinner guest list and a subsequent Secret Service investigation focused on security procedures, Rogers headed back to Chicago under a cloud.

But Rogers's network delivered. Her good friend Linda Johnson Rice, owner of Johnson Publishing Company, selected Rogers to run her business. Now you can hardly open a newspaper without reading about Rogers and her success at rebuilding a business with an inimitable brand.

Nevertheless, Rogers remains fuel for the gossip mill because the powerful network she built includes those who let her go when the political times demanded it.

Rogers's fall and comeback is a cautionary tale. Here are the lessons I draw from it and other falls from grace:

★ The minute you've fallen say, "Thank you for the opportunity to serve." Keep saying it, remembering the advice in etiquette books: you can never say "thank you" too often.

★ If you're embarrassed, don't say so or offer up any public evidence of that embarrassment. I repeat: you are always honored to serve.

★ Talk only to your network about the next chance. Your network will lead you to others who can be helpful, if need be.

★ If you're at a loss as to what's next, don't hide and stew. Remain visible and ask your network to be visible with you. You should be able to expect their loyalty at all times.

★ If you could point the finger at someone else, resist the urge. You'll want that person aboard future campaigns.

★ If the position you worked so hard to get turns out not to be right for you, don't discuss that publicly until you've got a plan for the next position.

You might be thinking, how hard could it really have been for Rogers, what with her connections and all? But that's exactly the point: the higher you go, the farther there is to fall, and the more you need your network.

Rogers was featured in *Vogue*, the *Wall Street Journal*, and the *New York Times*. This visibility and the power of her network made regrouping all the more complicated. If she can grin and bear it, with the cameras flashing and the screaming headlines in view at every newsstand, so can you.

Here is another instructive aspect of Rogers's story: if your network got you into the position, don't embarrass your network when you lose it. And because the more politically important the members of your network are, the riskier it was for them to help you in the first place, you need a network bound to you in bonds of steel, not fine thread. In the Rogers's case, this meant her friend Linda Johnson Rice could help her when others couldn't.

As former UNICEF and Peace Corps director and current chair of the Global Partnership for Education, Carol Bellamy's network is as strong as Rogers's. Like Rogers's, her career trajectory makes it clear that no matter how well prepared you are, or how hard you work, or how good your network is at winning for you, sometimes you will lose badly and have to call on the network to regroup. Bellamy says that when she lost her race for mayor of New York City in 1985, "that was a bad loss." When she lost a statewide campaign, she took to heart what she had learned as a Peace Corps member working in a strange land: "Learn to fail without being a failure."

Politics is at least as strange a place as anywhere you might volunteer for the Peace Corps. When Bellamy reached another career turning point, she did not need to wonder what to do. It was back to her network. She was appointed director of the Peace Corps. Next up, she was appointed head of UNICEF. A powerful girlfriend, former secretary of state under Bill Clinton, Madeleine Albright, was key to the appointment.

I was surprised to hear from Bellamy that she "wasn't number one on the list" when a new job was available. But she got the job anyway, again calling on her network to make her case. This chapter in Bellamy's political career illustrates another truth about access to political power: those who possess it like to exercise it. Unless they do, who knows they've got it? Remember this whenever you want to get to the big boys and girls. Pick up that phone and call that gatekeeper or childhood friend or boyfriend or girlfriend. Odds are, he or she will be flattered you asked and glad for the chance to strut his or her stuff. The more you demonstrate your ability to open doors, the more rooms you get invited into, because the inviter knows you can help her, too. And the rooms get better and better. The next time you look at the guest list for a state dinner, forget what the women wore and focus on this instead: How can I get to know the people on that list?

Even though Barack Obama bested Hillary Clinton, winning the 2008 Democratic presidential nomination, he made an early call to her once he was elected president. He knew to protect his flanks: "Keep your friends close and your enemies closer."

When Ludmyrna "Myrna" Lopez ran for reelection to the city council of Richmond, California, in 2010, she lost but converted that experience into the opportunity to direct a program that benefited the women of her city council district. If she decides to run for public office again, she will be able to call on her newly expanded network for campaign help. Which brings me to another piece of important advice, offered by feminist activist Shelby Knox: if you lose a campaign, you're still in a good position. "You still have a public face; you know the media; you have a network of donors; you know the landscape for the next time; you know the issues." And, as Lopez did, you will have the chance to expand your network of decision makers who can make those important telephone calls in the next campaign.

These stories all prove that repeat wins are possible, even when you lose a big Election Day. But only if you are willing to pick yourself up and get moving. As you do, remember that if you live by the sword (for instance, you ask a colleague to make a telephone call on your behalf outside the formal selection process for the appointment you seek—happens all the time, by the way), be prepared to die (politically) by the sword. And remember that no one owes you anything. If you got the job because you had access to the decision makers, don't kvetch when other decision makers take it away. Your network is a mutual aid association. It doesn't exist only for your benefit. Unless you help others win their campaigns, they won't help you, much less call on the big boys and girls in their own networks.

When you've really screwed up, and there's no excuse for your mistake, there is always redemption. The world loves a sinner—the rest of us can feel better by comparison. Remember Bill Clinton. And while you're contemplating his glorious recovery from condemnation for tawdry behavior, remember that some in your network will need some redemption one day, too. Be prepared to supply it.

Strategic imperatives for weaving those bonds of steel:

★ Once your initial web of relationships is woven, take charge, and keep charge, of connecting one person to the next, so you are always the center of your network. That's where you can get the most help.

★ Because the big boys and big girls pride themselves on what their networks can do for others, do them a solid and let them boost you up.

★ Remember that it's fun to be connected to lots of people, to be engaged with their lives and work and families—and what they care about.

★ When you ask a friend for help, and she turns you down, remember this: it doesn't mean she doesn't care. She may be going through tough times, too. If you sense this, offer to help her, even if you are hurting. She will remember, and she may share news of this (wonderful) quality of yours with others. That's good for you. Besides, it will make you feel better.

The power of sisterhood

Even though former governor of Alaska Sarah Palin violently disagrees with Hillary Clinton on many issues, when Palin received the nomination to run for vice president alongside John McCain in his 2008 race against Barack Obama for president, she made a point of aligning herself with Clinton as a woman in her acceptance speech. "I think Senator Clinton showed a lot of determination and stick-to-it-iveness in her campaigns and I have to respect that. I don't have to agree with all that she tried to push through and parts of her agenda. In fact, I don't agree with all of it. But there are some things that Hillary Clinton did that nobody can take away from her. And that is the eighteen million cracks that she put there in that highest and hardest glass ceiling in America's political scene. She was able to affect that, and I respect that."

Palin was acknowledging a sisterhood that transcends policy to share interest in the betterment of society. Wars, crime, jobs, safety, childcare, schools, health care—"Every issue is a women's issue," says Cecile Richards. This statement is true not only because all issues affect all people, but also because every issue, like combating pay inequality or sexual violence, affects women uniquely.

The smart campaigner will acknowledge this sisterhood as well, and use it to get elected. Worried about being perceived as a "women's candidate"? This strategy will ensure that every woman perceives you as her ally. Last time I looked, that was half the population. Assuming you can get some men to vote for you, too, you've got it in the bag.

Your unifying message will demonstrate your ever-increasing inevitability as the person who should win. Then, when you do win, you'll govern with increasing influence and power, penetrating seemingly impenetrable barriers. You will pass important legislation and create important policies because the sisterhood is behind you.

Clearly, the public policy solutions to these common issues often differ—these days, often enormously. For instance, women candidates disagree on what the law should be regarding women's right to reproductive choice. Some see abortion in the same context as other health issues, as a matter for a woman and her doctor to evaluate. Others see abortion as murder, not as a medical procedure. Many businesswomen disagree with a commonly held position among women's issues advocates that government regulation should force them to offer equal pay or paid sick leave, even when women workers suffer most from the disparities.

My friends Illinois state representative Barbara Flynn Currie and US representative Jan Schakowsky, Currie's former colleague in the General Assembly, have both had success working across the political and legislative aisles on issues of general concern to all.

Schakowsky, former Democratic cochair of the Congressional Caucus for Women's Issues, can point to a list of federal bills the Congressional Caucus spearheaded that reflect the common interests of women: the Pregnancy Discrimination Act, the Child Support Enforcement Act, the Retirement Equity Act, the Women's Business Ownership Act, the Breast and Cervical Cancer Mortality Prevention Act, and the Family and Medical Leave Act.

Currie says it took many years to pass a piece of legislation about childcare that was very important to her (and other women legislators). Meanwhile, she achieved other victories working with the other women legislators. Currie developed a multifaceted, commonsense agenda that all kinds of other people could adopt. It might have been an agenda full of "girl bills," as Currie and Schakowsky joked when they were colleagues in the Illinois legislature, but those bills mattered to women's lives, and those girl bills built a sisterhood.

Currie says, "I also sponsored a bill that would have required the state to provide pay scales for its own employees that were set without regard to gender or race. We'd had a pilot study that showed that female and African American–dominated job classifications in state government employment paid less than those predominantly white and male. My bill would have required the state to establish wage parity, and it gave the state plenty of time—nine years—to make it happen." The bill also had a Republican sponsor, Karen Hasara, later mayor of Springfield, Illinois, the state capital. "Jan spoke passionately for the bill," Currie continues. "It passed the house and senate but was vetoed by the governor."

Congresswoman Schakowsky told me she congratulated fellow congresswoman Michele Bachmann after her run for the presidency. Schakowsky approached Bachman, a politician who is Schakowsky's polar opposite on virtually every public policy matter, on the House of Representatives floor and said, "Though we disagree on most things, I want you to know that the self-confidence you showed in the presidential debates, and the courage to get out there [and run] is inspiring to women."

Louisiana state senator Sharon Broome says women officials' views on policy or legislation "should not divide us regarding wanting to empower women."

Melanne Verveer, appointed by President Obama as the first US ambassador-at-large for global women's issues and founding executive director of the Georgetown University Institute for Women, Peace and Security, says, "If women in elected office can work together across partisan lines, even where their numbers are not large, they can have considerable impact in bringing to the table issues that need to be addressed but would not have otherwise. For example, in the US Congress women have led the way on a range of issues from Title IX to a law to combat domestic violence—with the support of their male colleagues."

Verveer traveled the world with former Secretary of State Clinton, promoting a pro-women, all-women-are-sisters, sisterhood-is-powerful agenda. The purpose of the State Department office she created is "to ensure that women's issues are fully integrated in the formulation and conduct of US foreign policy," according to the State Department's website. It "works to promote stability, peace, and development by empowering women politically, socially, and economically around the world."

"After meeting with women members of Congress and hearing what they had achieved through bipartisan legislation," Verveer says, "a Kuwaiti woman who was struggling to gain the right to vote and stand for office for women in Kuwait remarked, 'Imagine what we could do in our country if women could hold elective office.'"

Verveer says, "In so many ways, women bring crucial leadership, talent, and skills to public policy and society. If women can come together on some of these common issues . . ."

I asked Ambassador Verveer whether sisterhood gets us beyond profound disagreements about policy solutions in a way that is more than just rhetorical. Is any woman better than no woman at the political leadership table?

"It's an issue of fairness," she answered. "Decisions shouldn't be made by only half the population. We shortchange women and public policy when the experiences, talents, and perspectives of women are not tapped in policymaking."

Verveer says more women at the table means there's a better chance issues of concern to women will be addressed. She says more women in positions of political leadership means greater economic prosperity, because their leadership exemplifies women's right to be on high rungs of the economic ladder. And women leaders beget other women leaders, in numbers that make a difference.

"Women are on the front lines of change, playing leadership roles," she says. "One night in Afghanistan in a conversation with several Afghan women, one of them pleaded, 'Please do not look at us as victims, but see us as the leaders that we are.'"

Verveer goes on, "The World Economic Forum's annual gender gap report measures the gap between men and women in a given country on four metrics: access to education, health and survivability, political empowerment, and economic participation. In countries where the gap between men and women is closer to being closed in the four areas, those countries are more prosperous and economically competitive."

In other words, she says, "Investing in women is one of the most effective investments that can be made to advance political, economic, and social progress around the globe. Investing in women improves the world. It is not just the right thing to do but the smart thing as well."

Verveer was chief of staff to First Lady Hillary Clinton and a close ally during Clinton's failed campaign for the Democratic Party presidential nomination in 2008. She knows about the power of sisterhood in the bad times, as well as the good.

On the campaign trail, your acknowledgment of sisterhood will broaden your network of supporters.

When I was a student living in Chicago, a friend gave me the book *Sisterhood Is Powerful*. This bible has been at my side ever since. As I've fought for women's empowerment, I've used the lessons from this book. It teaches us that regardless of where any American woman lives, she is part of the sisterhood. Whether she's a Republican or a Democrat, she will have to fight the same battles to beat the boys to become a public leader. Because sisterhood is powerful as a fact of life, it can be powerful as a shaper of life.

This doesn't mean that political women shouldn't be—or aren't—concerned about what Currie and Schakowsky called "boys' bills," but it does mean that if you're planning your strategy for winning on Election Day, you should remember that this sisterhood created around a set of women's issues may account for a broad swath of supporters across party lines, and for the depth of commitment you will receive from them.

Verveer also told me about a meeting she attended with a group of Latin American women politicos who meet once a month. They ran the gamut from socialists to diehard conservatives. According to Verveer, they explained this by saying, "We disagree on many issues among us, but we've also learned to come together across party divisions on key issues and create progress together."

Strategic imperatives for harnessing the power of sisterhood:

★ Call upon it.

★ If you invite all your sisters into your corner, that corner could become as big as Times Square.

★ The more women you consider your allies simply by virtue of sisterhood, the more women there are in your corner.

★ Sisterhood is as powerful as brotherhood. Proclaim the power of your sisterhood in the halls where the big boys are seated.

★ Sisterhoods are built just like Avon Lady parties and can be equally all-inclusive.

★ Have some parties of the sisterhood and for the sisterhood.

—| PART III |—

YOU CAN NEVER CARE TOO MUCH

21

When you're working, there are no volunteers, there is no free lunch, and there sure isn't any coffee break

Volunteering is a misnomer—anything you devote time to is work, whether you get paid or not. When deciding whether or not to volunteer, you assess your need or desire to do the work. You consider every work-related lunch invitation in light of what you can achieve at that lunch. And whether even your breaks, coffee or otherwise, will advance your campaign. Of course you'll also kick back and have coffee or lunch with a friend, or exercise to preserve your health and sanity, or celebrate holidays with friends or family. But try to keep in mind that Hillary Clinton didn't stop being secretary of state to plan her daughter Chelsea's wedding. She did both. Monica Banks didn't stop being chancery clerk when she became an associate minister of her husband's church. You'll find ways to juggle, too, if you want to win on Election Day.

Carol Bellamy, chair of the Global Partnership for Education, finishes her workout by 7:30 AM. Then it's off to her desk to "do Europe," or, rather, to conduct business with colleagues overseas, whose day is already half over. She follows those calls with calls to successively earlier time zones across the United States.

Bellamy began working early on for the Democratic Party, putting herself in position to be drafted. "I became president of my local [political] club," she says, "Then they needed someone to fill out the ticket." She was chosen by her local Democratic Party club to run for the New York state senate: fortune gifted the well prepared.

"I like to work. I work hard. I take things seriously. I prepare," says Bellamy. "Roll your sleeves up."

Not that she liked all the work she had to do. "I'd go out and do the pools in Brighton Beach," she says, recalling meeting voters at local swimming pools. "Do I really want to do this? No. But then, just do. Grit your teeth. Tighten your fists."

By the time she was thirty-five, Bellamy was president of the New York City Council, the second most powerful person in the city government. She distinguished herself in that role in part by focusing on the welfare of foster children. Work that began in her city council office is the subject of a recently published book by David Tobis, *From the Other Side: How Parents and Their Allies Changed New York City's Child Welfare System*.

However, Bellamy's career as an elected official was over by the time she was fifty, after she lost a race for New York State comptroller. She had years in front of her to work, and she had a ton of valuable experience. She was prepared for a new career, but where to turn?

The volunteering Bellamy had done in other people's campaigns, as a member of her local political club, and in national campaigns to increase the number of women elected officials, and the advice she'd given over countless lunches, had built up a store of goodwill and put Bellamy in a position to call her friends and ask for help.

Thus began phase two of Bellamy's political career. When the top job at the Peace Corps became available, Bellamy told the *Milwaukee Journal Sentinel*, "Donna pushed hard for me." "Donna" was her friend Donna Shalala, who at the time was the secretary of the US Department of Health and Human Services.

Later, when the job of executive director of UNICEF opened up, Bellamy says, Madeleine Albright "came up to me and said, 'How about being our candidate?'"

Bellamy has won many awards and honors since then, including the Medal of Distinction from Barnard College, an honorary degree from Bates College, and the Order of the Rising Sun, which was created by Emperor Meiji of Japan in 1875 to recognize extraordinary public service.

As head of the Global Partnership for Education, which puts together partnerships of "donor and low income countries," Bellamy recently led an effort to raise $1.5 billion to fund children's education around the world.

With a career like that, you have to wonder which came first, the personality or the work demanding that kind of dedication? Maybe both. You may be tempted to dismiss Bellamy and others like her as workaholics. Let others use that disparaging term while they sit and complain about how their public officials are letting them down.

If you want to be one of the people making those decisions, you need to be like Bellamy. There is a lot to do, and the only way to win is to do it. If you do, you'll be able to take pride in what you accomplish.

Reflecting on her career, Justice Kimball says, "I gave speeches all over—anytime anyone asked me."

Recollecting her own long-shot first run for legislative office, New Jersey state representative Caroline Casagrande says, it "was won on shoe leather. Every day after work, I put on my khakis and sneakers and did my 'walk list' for that day—April through October."

Rain or shine. Hot or cold. If you follow these examples, if you're willing to put everything you've got into your campaign, and if you're ready for some double shifts, you too will be well positioned when a fortuitous opening comes up.

Once I put in a call to Bellamy at her office, and she called me back a few minutes later as she walked down a noisy New York City street. Four decades on, Bellamy fit in the callback at her first opportunity. She didn't even wait to get back to the office. Her stellar political career is proof that this "no coffee break" mentality can create a life that is as exhilarating as the free time you're opting out of.

The Monday before the 2008 presidential election, Deanna Archuleta was on the phone with a colleague musing about who might be picked for the Obama transition team. While on the telephone, she received an e-mail inviting her to be a member.

A donor to an organization Archuleta had previously directed was in the room when the selection committee was puzzling over the slot. "They wanted diversity," Archuleta says, "a woman conservationist with experience in local office." The donor remembered Archuleta, who fit the bill. "Who in the world doesn't want to serve on that transition team?" Archuleta says. She thought, So what if I have to work all day every day for free for six weeks? So what if there won't be any breaks, coffee or otherwise? So what if I have to ask my parents to move in and take care of the children and then pay my own way to DC and my own room and board while I'm there? She knew this would be a small step in terms of the investments she'd have to make but a giant leap along her path to Election Day. Just like the step she took when she became president of the PTA and her neighborhood association simultaneously, in order to make sure neighborhood children could cross the street safely on their way to school.

Mary Landrieu, the senior US senator from Louisiana, began her career in elected office in much the same way Bellamy and Casagrande did, with election to the state legislature. Landrieu was twenty-five when she first ran. She moved on to be elected twice as state treasurer. Then it was on to the US Senate at age forty-one.

Landrieu agrees that every day is Election Day: "It's very true. It's 24/7. Sometimes, it's difficult to separate private life from public life. I don't work every minute of every day, [but] in the course of conversation, I don't say, 'I'm not working today.' In that way, every day is Election Day. People are sizing you up every day." When it came to the 2012 Democratic National Convention, Landrieu was not to be found in Charlotte, North Carolina. She was back home, helpfully dealing with the fallout of Hurricane Isaac—back home where her voters are sizing her up for re-election in 2014.

Every year for the past twenty-five, my husband and I have attended the New Orleans Jazz and Heritage Festival, which features a variety of music from all over the world. Along with the food tents and the craft tents there is a book tent where you can buy the best books about

Louisiana—on its politics as well as its music and food. Not long ago I was speaking with the young woman behind the book tent cash register about women in politics. "I always knew it was possible, but I needed to see somebody doing it," she said, describing Hillary Clinton's presidential run.

Who are you tracking? Watch her holding fast to her dream; start working for campaigns, as she undoubtedly did, and start filling your coffee break time befriending other women who agree that women need to grab more opportunities in politics. These women can become your campaign workers. Start taking important women to lunch and sharing your dream with them—and make sure they know how hard you are willing to work for it.

That lunch won't be free, no matter who picks up the check. Politics is a game of exchanging favors or, expressed more delicately, doing unto others as you would have them do unto you. Consequently, don't lunch with anyone you're not willing to help as much as you want that person to help you.

I always advise building your lunch schedule the way you would build a house. The foundation is first. The decorating is last. Which lunch companions can help you build your foundation? That's who you'll invite to lunch first.

Here are some ways to think about your approach to your busy days:

- ★ I can't wait to get started.
- ★ I'm free Saturday morning.
- ★ I'm happy to distribute fliers.
- ★ I love going to new places and meeting new people.
- ★ My partner would enjoy coming, too.

Strategic imperatives for happily becoming a no-coffee-break kind of girl:

- ★ You are enamored of the position you are seeking.

★ Your family and friends are equally enamored because they know achieving your goal will make you happy.

★ You find ways to take personal breaks that aren't anxiety-producing; for example, you exercise a lot, or you regularly get together with your BFF, or you engage in retail therapy—within your means, of course.

★ You summon strength even when you're exhausted because the power of your dream keeps you moving forward.

22

How helping others will help you

Constantly showing, and, more important, acting on your concern for others is a simple and effective way to distinguish yourself from the candidates who show up at the soup kitchen once a year (usually at Thanksgiving). Serving others is good for its own sake, but it also serves you.

My friend Laura Washington, a political reporter in Chicago, occasionally hosts dinners for her colleagues and political-junkie pals. Though the gatherings often feature a conversation with a journalist, one night in 2011 the guest was Toni Preckwinkle, longtime Chicago City Council member and newly elected president of the Cook County Board of Commissioners. The restaurant was overflowing: Preckwinkle's report about her first months in office was a hot ticket. If you'd asked any one of us in attendance if we'd predicted that Preckwinkle, a longtime independent actor in a game that mostly rewards insiders, would win this office, we'd have said the odds were about the same as the odds she'd land on Mars.

I have a box full of campaign buttons next to my computer documenting a life working on worthy but doomed political campaigns for fabulous women who wanted to do good. For some of Preckwinkle's admirers, hers was the worthiest, and that dinner felt like a victory celebration. A good guy had won. Better yet, the good guy was a girl.

The job she'd won wouldn't be a cakewalk. The president of the Cook County Board of Commissioners is responsible for the jails, the public health system, and many of the problems of the nation's third-largest city. Because Cook County includes 40 percent of the residents of the state of Illinois, many of the state's problems land on her desk as well.

The reason Preckwinkle is the good guy, and the reason I supported her, is that she has sought public office because she wanted to be a public servant.

"There are historic injustices that need remedying," she says. "The jails are the intersection of racism and poverty." When was the last time you heard a politician utter a sentence like that?

During the Q&A session following drinks and dinner, someone pointed out that public service is not top of mind for a lot of politicians—that would be getting reelected or planning a run for higher office—and asked Preckwinkle why she likes electoral politics. She said she has liked the politics, as well as the policy, ever since she was a teenager, when she volunteered in 1964 in the campaign of another African American woman, Katherine McWatt, the first African American woman to run for the city council in Preckwinkle's hometown of Saint Paul, Minnesota. Preckwinkle learned then that in political campaigns, "There is camaraderie and a lot of fun; a date certain when it's done." She calls politics "the ultimate team sport. It's a common cause that's important; politics is where it [collective social action] matters the most."

McWatt was a teacher, as is Preckwinkle. "I'm a teacher by profession, and it's a profession I'm very proud of," she says. I've heard her say many times on the political stump that she is "a history teacher with a temp job." At the dinner, she explained a connection: "Politics is a process of teaching people to learn and adopt your view."

However, politics Saint Paul–style is one thing. Politics Chicago-style is quite another. Chicago, not Saint Paul, has a reputation as home base for political hardball. Most of the players here are also men who have been on the team and in the clubhouse for decades. As ward committeeman Timothy O'Sullivan famously said to Abner Mikva, former counsel to president Bill Clinton and federal Appeals Court judge, when Mikva tried to volunteer to work on Adlai Stevenson's presidential campaign, "We don't want nobody nobody sent."

Preckwinkle didn't let this stop her. During her 1991 city council campaign, she sought and received the help of John Stroger, a long-time Democratic Party regular who would later precede her as Cook County Board president. And just as she had in Saint Paul, Preckwinkle went to work in other people's campaigns.

Once she decided she had learned enough, she ran for city council, only succeeding on her third try.

Preckwinkle was an alderman for nineteen years, governing about fifty-five thousand constituents in a South Side ward. During her tenure, she built a reputation for taking the public service side of the job seriously. She was constantly moving and helping out. She schooled herself in all kinds of policy matters. She developed her own policy proposals and advocated for them. She organized her neighbors to fight for her proposals to address the ward's problems: a dearth of jobs, poor housing, bad schools, and rampant crime. There seemed no problem too small, no meeting too small to discuss the problem, no group too odd, no cause too marginal, to merit Preckwinkle's attention. She made sure that when her constituents needed city services, they got them. Preckwinkle describes the work this way: "Everything I worked on was what my community needed, and what I believed in."

A guest at the dinner asked Preckwinkle about her years in the city council: What part of it had she liked best? Preckwinkle responded, "You're like the mayor of your little town—responsible for everyone. I like that."

She built a political organization to accomplish her goals. "You have to find your own team. It takes putting your own organization together. If you decide to stand up and don't put your own organization together, you're fair game. You'll have perceived weaknesses other people see as opportunity."

Preckwinkle recruited community residents to be campaign workers. She trained them in political organizing and hosted motivational gatherings. Periodically, she hosts a weekend breakfast for her workers. From this base, she develops alliances with other politicians who can be helpful to her, just as she is to them. There are needy people everywhere. Time for you to get moving and help out, too.

Voters like politicians who take responsibility for them. At a minimum, a candidate has to say she cares, show up, and then do something, but you're probably more like Preckwinkle. You actually do care. You actually like being able to help out and take responsibility. Perhaps, also like Preckwinkle, you've been doing this for a while. Perhaps you are now wondering, How do I know my Election Day will ever come?

You don't. But, if you do as Preckwinkle does—if you are the "mayor" of your community, responsible for as many good works as you possibly can be—you will be able to claim everyone to your side when your time comes. Preckwinkle says she was willing to wait until the right job came along. So should you.

If you start your political career in the spirit of doing good, you will eventually win because people want good people taking care of them.

It might take you several tries to win, as it did for Preckwinkle. So what? After that, Preckwinkle was mayor of her own little city for almost twenty years.

It might be tough getting there. For instance, when I asked Preckwinkle what running for Cook County Board president was like, she said, "It was excruciating, especially the fund-raising part. I don't know why I didn't give up." But she didn't, and once the major newspapers endorsed her she was able to raise enough money for a television ad—opening with a photo of teacher Preckwinkle with this line: "I taught high school." A month later she was elected, president of more than five million people.

I asked her whether she really liked having to keep moving, three decades on. Maybe she's getting tired. Maybe she has just disciplined herself to keep turning out and helping out because she has a holy war she wants to win. Not at all, she says. She loves her work. She has said she is planning to run again.

Strategic imperatives for helping out:

★ Constantly act on your concern for others. This is the quickest way to distinguish yourself from the mass of would-be candidates.

★ "Resist being something you're not, because it makes you inauthentic to yourself," says Preckwinkle.

★ Appreciate the importance of the political process and engaging others in it.

★ Don't ever be too good to do what needs doing, however unpleasant or menial, for whoever needs it.

★ Be the leader of your group that goes where help is needed, and take responsibility for making sure it gets done right.

★ Don't ever say you're tired.

★ Don't wait to be asked.

23

Show you care

"**W**here's Becca?" When I hear Jan Schakowsky's voice, especially her voice using my baby name, I feel warm inside, and I bet that's the way a lot of people feel about her. That's because Schakowsky, one of Illinois's representatives in Congress and a cochair of President Obama's reelection campaign in 2012, is usually talking about issues that matter to people in the most personal ways. Some that jump to mind are: jobs, health care, food and toy safety, and racial and gender equality. Her manner is always warm, personal, direct, and interested.

Unlike US senators, who have six years to make their case for reelection, or statewide elected officials, who usually have four, US representatives have to ask for the order every couple of years.

Schakowsky freely admits that the majority of her constituents (congressional districts usually hold around six hundred thousand people) share her political views and therefore her district "affords me the opportunity to be an unequivocal voice." But she also says "that's who I am," to explain how she manages to work on such a wide range of issues. "If I really do believe in something, I feel like I have to be true to those convictions. There's a consistency about it, a relationship among all the issues. Voters can then decide every two years whether to throw me out."

There are the big donors who gave yesterday and want today, the constituents who voted yesterday and demand today, and the VIPs who ask, "What have you done for me lately?" How does she keep them all happy? By caring about everything. Then everyone has a chance to think positively about something.

Why does Schakowsky operate this way when she only needs 50 percent plus one to win in a district where her voters generally agree with her? Because sometimes they don't. And there's always someone else who wants the job.

As you can probably guess, Schakowsky doesn't have much in the way of downtime. You want what she's having?

Schakowsky says her personal test of how she's doing is how she's received at her neighborhood Jewel grocery store. People will confront you about their issues pretty much anywhere.

Schakowsky's public career started in a Jewel supermarket aisle. She told the story to the *Feministing* blog: "When I was a very young house-wife a group of us got together because we wanted to know how old our food was." They couldn't tell because the manufacturers were using codes to indicate the dates on the packages. "The six of us called our-selves 'National Consumers United' and we took on the food industry. . . . You can imagine as a very young woman what an empowering experience that was. . . . I mark that as the creation story, the beginning of my view of myself as someone who could be part of changing the world."

Note that she viewed herself as "someone who could be part of changing the world," not someone who would track food labeling for the rest of her life. You won't be a single-issue person all your life either. Think about it: while you're protesting human rights violations down-town, people are still going to bed hungry in your neighborhood.

After Schakowsky cofounded National Consumers United she became program director of Illinois Public Action, director of the Illinois State Council of Senior Citizens, and a state legislator for eight years. After her congressional district's member of the US House of Representatives retired, she won his office and has served since 1999.

Schakowsky's training as a community organizer while at Illinois Public Action has come in handy in public office, as community organizing teaches you how to be a leader with a strategy and a message, not a leader with a management plan. She has built a multifaceted issue agenda and a power base to align with it. Community organizers are taught to approach policy and political change fearlessly. This means confronting the opposition and making a lot of public noise, if that's what's needed to win. They're trained to size up situations quickly, so the opportunity to make a change is not lost. They're also taught to move adeptly from solving one problem to solving the next. And they are taught that if you can't solve the first problem, you don't let that deter you from moving on to the second one. If you have to compromise to get a win, Schakowsky says, "The question is, on balance, are we moving forward? You work as hard as you can, and take the victory."

As to Schakowsky's issues: Could you rank them in importance? Could you say that access to food is more important than access to housing? Or that preventing domestic violence is more important than preventing rape? A leader has to make choices. Focusing on all issues equally at the same time leads to confusion, or sinking to the lowest common denominator, or failing to take advantage of moments when important breakthroughs are at hand. Playing favorites is always a dangerous game, but that doesn't mean you should give equal amounts of your time to each. You could say that, because of your own experience, or a family member's, or a friend's, you are compelled to focus on one more than the others, or that because of a unique set of circumstances, you are only focused on one at the moment but you still care about them all. You always care about all of them.

After Schakowsky won her first primary, she says, "I met with my kitchen cabinet. We thought I had to choose between a leadership position and being a progressive leader. Turns out, I can be both a leader in the Democratic Caucus and a progressive leader. There aren't that many organizers in Congress. My office is a place where inside/outside strategies get developed"—meaning campaigns including two advocacy components: one among elected officials and one among community residents.

Schakowsky's success at being a progressive voice beyond her district means Schakowsky's platform has gotten bigger and bigger. Those successes in Congress include her leadership role in passage of the Affordable Care Act, and according to her official biography, "provisions in the laws that protect seniors from abusive terms in reverse mortgages, require greater transparency for military contractors, require the strongest possible mandatory safety standards and testing for infant and toddler products—including high chairs, cribs, and bath seats—and also that require strict car safety measures to protect children."

Schakowsky now appears regularly as a commentator on national TV news shows. When she does, she demonstrates that she cares about health care and jobs and other issues every viewer thinks about. Schakowsky says, "Women now come up to me in airport bathrooms."

And what's all this done for her profile as a candidate? Well, being visible and being caring and being known for caring mean more and more people want to vote for you, a good thing for a person running for office every couple of years.

In 2010 Schakowsky faced a serious competitor in the general election. He disagreed with her (positive) position toward creating a Palestinian state. Schakowsky won handily, perhaps because one controversial issue wasn't enough to undermine her general profile as someone her district can trust. "My constituents are like family to me," is how Schakowsky puts it. See how she did that?

Strategic imperatives for showing you care:

★ Among the many issues you care about, periodically select a few to be the center of your advocacy program, and then connect all the others you take on with those. That way your agenda won't appear scattered, while it still covers everything you want it to cover.

★ Create a profile that celebrates this connected agenda. (Schakowsky's tagline is "Put a fighter on your side.")

★ Make noise when it's needed. Once, when the powerful Illinois congressman Dan Rostenkowski was advocating reducing Medicare benefits, Schakowsky and her senior citizens' group chased him down the street.

★ Bring the media out to watch your noise making and listen to your victory speech. Once, Rachel Durchslag and her colleagues drummed up a letter-writing campaign against a bar when it hosted a "pimps and hos" party.

★ Don't play favorites with issues because you like certain people better than others.

★ Always answer your phone, even if you're frantically busy. You don't want the caller to assume, which she will, that you don't care about her or her cause.

★ If you aren't winning on all your issues, frame your progress like a ball player: talk about how you're succeeding one hit at a time. That's how you will win the game.

24

You can get access to anyone, and anyone can become a convert to your cause

The saying goes that there are only six degrees of separation between any two people on Earth. As you continuously build and strengthen your relationships, this will become easier to see. Start by thinking of those relationships as product endorsements and yourself as the product. And just as with products, an endorsement from a celebrity or a VIP will work wonders for your ability to gather other votes. The higher the value of your endorsers, the easier it'll be to convince others to support you.

At the beginning of my political career, I had trouble with this. Why couldn't my work, or the work of a friend, or of a client, be sufficient to elicit an endorsement from a VIP? Well, it might, but you can't win unless you get the majority of the votes, and the better your endorsements, the more votes you'll likely get.

And don't get hung up on thinking that VIPs are only celebrities who live in New York or Los Angeles. Is there a popular soccer coach in your community? How about the president of the League of Women Voters, or the head of a local businesswomen's group? No matter where you live or at what rung you start to climb the ladder of public leadership, there will be people around you who can make that climb easier and faster. Barack Obama got Scarlett Johansson and Eva Longoria and Kerry Washington, but you don't have to. Not yet, anyway.

Think creatively as you make your list of prospective endorsers. Answer these questions about each prospect as you develop your list: Is the woman well liked by a broad swath of those you seek to convert to your cause? Is she admired in different voting blocs, not just one? Is the woman well spoken, with an optimistic style? Is the woman the sort who is willing to go the extra mile—in good spirits—to get the job done? If she's high maintenance, does her endorsement value outweigh the drag of dealing with her sometimes unreasonable requests? Is the woman adventurous about engaging in unfamiliar projects? Do you need this woman to win your current race, or are you better off saving her for later, when you have bigger fish to fry or when her endorsement will create ripples in a bigger pond? And last but really first: Will you be able to quickly get to that woman and convince her that you are a winner?

If you answered yes to these questions, keep that woman on your list. Then go get her.

Dozens of times I've found that either I or someone in my close network can get to an endorser I want to reach. Sometimes, I have to go with that endorser's gatekeeper. That works, too. Sometimes I strike out, but I go up to bat again.

I was a young political organizer when I first saw this process in action, working with the actor Carol Burnett. She had an enormously popular prime-time variety show, and she was eager to be a women's advocate. The actor Alan Alda, known for his role on M*A*S*H, was a supporter of the National Women's Political Caucus (NWPC). He called Burnett to ask her to get involved in the NWPC campaign to ratify the Equal Rights Amendment. Illinois was a high-priority state, and I was charged with organizing Burnett's media and lobbying tour; so I got to work lining up local VIPs.

My job was to bring them into the cause supported by Alda and Burnett, but along the way I got them on board with me as well. If you're working for a cause, whether you're campaigning for someone else or for yourself, you are the one building the connections.

For those few days in 1976, I watched Burnett get pulled in because a friend called a friend who called a friend. I got it fast and decided I could build that sort of network, too. I didn't need to begin in Hollywood; my field of dreams was Chicago, and I knew Chicago was full of people who could endorse me, making a difference to my political future. And they would lead me to their friends, and they to their friends, and someday I'd be in Hollywood, too, if that's what I needed to move forward. From then on, if I calculated that I needed the support of celebrities, I figured out who would be on the chain, who was the friend talking to a friend talking to a friend for this campaign? I asked myself if I was ready to ask the biggest person on my list to join my cause, or whether I was still on hold with her.

You can't buy the kind of media attention the participation of a committed endorser creates. And they like that attention. They are in the business of being well known (they couldn't do their jobs if they weren't). If your cause reflects well on her, she will ask her friends and colleagues to help you out, too. Maybe one of them is a bigger fish. Bingo. If she has agents or publicists, she may ask them to help you out. Then you're really rolling.

Carol Burnett's publicist was so pleased with our joint campaign that he offered me a job. That wasn't what I wanted, but I loved the validation of the hard work I had put in, and it enabled me to approach the next similar process with confidence.

Another time, Cybill Shepherd was dating a political fund-raiser friend. He asked her to be in a documentary I was coproducing on the politics of abortion. She agreed enthusiastically, lending her movie star looks and considerable commitment to women's reproductive equality to a desperately important feature on women's health. Another time I recruited the renowned singer Mavis Staples to star in an ad campaign promoting participation in the US Census. I reached her through a friend's father. When I sought the endorsement of a Chicago mayor, one of those American Jewish Committee women I worked with in my first job was able to arrange the introduction, and

I got that endorsement with a really good pitch letter and a few telephone calls.

Work hard on those pitch letters. VIPs and celebrities have a lot on their plate, and you may only get one shot. They can also be high maintenance, perhaps as a result. While I'm a great admirer of Betty Friedan's heroic advocacy for women's equality, can I tell you about the time I barely found a hairdresser fast enough to suit her? I felt like my head was on the chopping block for that half hour. Another time, another celebrity—this one I could only speak to through her hairdresser! Apparently, the hairdresser's boss only talked to God. No matter. I gritted my teeth, vented privately to a couple of girlfriends, and kept in mind how important that celebrity's endorsement would be to my client's cause.

Big fish in small ponds can behave badly, too. But you're going to ignore bad behavior in pursuit of your larger goal. All of us have our bad (hair) days. Sometimes, no matter how much gel goes on the hair, it's still frizzy. I'm thinking that was how Betty Friedan felt that day when she had that temper tantrum right before my very eyes. Why did she want to go to the hairdresser so badly? Well, because she cared about my larger goal, and she wanted to look right when she met it. That was all good. I say accommodate those VIP requests and ignore bad treatment. If you're treated well, say thank you over and over again. In either case, you have a larger goal to achieve.

The minute an endorser accepts my, or a friend's, request, I share the good news to compound the benefits of her participation. Everyone the campaign knows, or sort of knows, is advised immediately. Leadership donors are asked to give again to fund spin-off opportunities. Leadership volunteers are asked to write personal thank-you notes. They are asked to spread the good news among their colleagues, which precipitates additional endorsements, which will also be critical to the success of the campaign. And they create buzz throughout the network, which translates into votes.

I hope I've convinced you by now that no matter how wonderful you think you are, that is no substitute for others saying how wonderful you are.

Strategic imperatives for lining up big-name supporters:

★ Make an inventory of any VIP connections to your family members, colleagues, and friends. Include in the inventory their contact information, information regarding their interests, and who else has received their endorsements.

★ If you know those other recipients, add them to your list of contacts for your campaign; maybe they can put in a good word for you.

★ Keep the contact information up to date. There's nothing worse than missing an opportunity to make a connection because you can't find a phone number you know you had but didn't record.

★ Pay attention to the media coverage of those you want to be your endorsers. Take it into account when you make a request.

★ Always stage your asks in accordance with impact, so that you don't waste an ask on something too small.

★ Make a wish list of VIPs you'd love to reach. Whenever you see contact information for them, or descriptions of their interests, add that information to your database. Keep track of the reasons they might consider endorsing you.

★ Make a speculative map of how you might reach these people so you can seize any opportunities that might present themselves.

★ Most of all: Don't be deterred by organizational charts or other tactics designed to discourage you from going straight to the top. All you want to do is make your case. Don't let anything get in the way of that goal.

25

That "having it all" thing

T ens of thousands of American women choose to run for public office every year. Tens of thousands of others seek political appointments. Add thousands of staff people and campaign workers and political consultants, and that's a whole lot of women working in politics—all toward their very own Election Days. We can only guess at the number who don't run for office because of personal deterrents like partners and children.

The women I spoke to for this book all have people who matter to them and a desire to have a personal life. Yet, they all decided that their personal lives would affirm and support their personal and political goals.

When Illinois attorney general Lisa Madigan was questioned about the possibility that she might hold higher office in the future, about whether she could hold a political job like governor simultaneous with being a mom, she said to the *Chicago Sun-Times*, "All of these jobs are very demanding. And people who, unfortunately, have to work three jobs and don't necessarily have health-care coverage—they're even in a worse situation. So nobody needs to give any pity on what elected officials have to endure."

Single mom Lori Healey, former chief of staff to Chicago mayor Richard M. Daley, declined a promotion when her children were in high school. "I've said no to a couple of things because of timing," she says. "But I never said no to anything because I didn't think I was up to it."

Deanna Archuleta was asked about her interest in running for office when she returned to New Mexico after serving in the first Obama administration. She told me her younger son is still in high school. "I'd like to get him launched." She is also a newlywed. However, Archuleta remains active in her community. For instance, in lieu of wedding gifts, she asked friends to make gifts to a local preschool for at-risk children and their families.

At age thirty-six, Molly Bordonaro served under George W. Bush as ambassador to Malta, where, she says, "I did a lot of interviews about being an ambassador and a mom because it was personally important to me . . . to use my position to help young Maltese women feel empowered."

Bordonaro ran for Congress at age twenty-seven. Had she won, she would have been the youngest woman ever elected. "My motivating experience was that I want to do something" in public policy, she says. "I'm not going to just complain without being proactive."

Bordonaro had recently returned to her hometown of Portland, Oregon, after working in DC as a public affairs consultant. She dove into the local political pool, running in the Republican primary against a sitting metro councilor. She "won in a landslide," she says, though she lost the general election narrowly.

Caroline Casagrande first ran for office much earlier than she thought she might because there were political discussions she wanted to be part of and policies she wanted to help shape. In particular, she was concerned about taxes and economic development. Even though she first dreamed of running for office when she was ten, she says, "I didn't think I would run at twenty-nine! You have your career, make your money; when things settle down, then you'll run."

Since her first campaign, Casagrande has had two children. She says it is important to run while you're a mother, to "show women who have a family that it is possible."

However, she also points out that motherhood has probably held her back professionally. When Casagrande returned to the New Jersey legislature only nine days after a C-section, a male colleague asked her, "How can you be here?"

"I serve with many men who've had many children," Casagrande says. "I'm sure it has limited me since they said out loud that they were concerned about my time. So you can imagine what they think."

She laughs out loud as she describes the piles of laundry she ignores on her way to political meetings. "You do the best you can," she says, adding that her children "are very good grounding for even the best office in the world. . . . They are such a blessing. I get to do both things in one day—put on my suit and pull them on the swing."

There's no question: working in politics can take you away from home, often for days or weeks at a time. Not everyone understands a woman who would want such a job. And it gets harder when you're married and a mother. Lisa Madigan acknowledges, "It's so much easier running for office when you're single; nobody missed me for dinner."

Lisa Madigan says that when she became a mother, she sought advice from political experts and made sure she would understand how voters, especially other mothers, would view her, because research suggests that women with young families are harshest against young women with families running for office.

"I always wanted a family," she says. "When I got pregnant, after telling my family, the next person I called was [my campaign pollster] Celinda Lake."

In addition to the considerable political support she received from her powerful parents, Madigan needed the support of the new family she was starting with her husband, Pat Byrnes, who writes and draws cartoons for the *New Yorker*. As a couple they made choices, she says, "His career had to give way to mine." Byrnes makes it work; he started a cartoon-filled blog, *Captain Dad*, which is the centerpiece of a forthcoming book.

Plenty of women in office have stay-at-home spouses or partners or parents or relatives who help make their demanding jobs work. Friends of Louisiana state senator and senate president pro tempore Sharon Broome introduced her to a man with three children who lived in Texas when her political career was already well under way. They decided to marry. A friend asked Broome whether she'd be quitting. No way. Instead, Broome's new husband and his three children moved to Baton Rouge. Adjustments were needed, of course: "I had to manage my leadership style for the home. I had to build unity. Our youngest son was eleven years old at the time. I was going through that!"

Before he passed away in 2007, Barbara Flynn Currie's husband, David Currie, a law professor, worked on all of Currie's campaigns, covering his precincts "always by bicycle." She was able to make family life work, she says, partly because Margaret, her teenage daughter, "assumed a lot of responsibility." Upon reflection, she says, she concluded there really wasn't anything wrong with that.

Of course marriage and political life won't work if you don't clue your partner in on the size of your ambitions or if he or she isn't committed to helping you achieve them. Deanna Archuleta, whose mother, she says, "had us walking and knocking on doors for candidates," says her first husband didn't understand how much her dream of holding office meant to her. When she first ran for county commissioner in Santa Fe, she says, he thought she would get it out of her system. She didn't. Eighteen months after she won, they were divorced.

"When you hold office," she continues. "Your family holds office. Make sure everyone is on the same page and has a full understanding of the demands of the particular office. Make sure you and your spouse are fully on board regarding the interruption of your personal life."

Archuleta moved to Washington for six weeks to serve on President Obama's 2008 transition team. Both of her parents moved into her New Mexico home to take care of her two boys. After the transition Archuleta was offered a permanent position in the Obama administration, so she and her children picked up and moved to Arlington, Virginia. When one son complained about the lack of diversity he expected to find there, Archuleta told her children about their new school: there were "110 first languages spoken there." Her boys were being given a once-in-a-lifetime opportunity, too.

Planned Parenthood's Laura Tucker says that when her three children were young, "I had a rule I won't be away from home more than two nights a week." But she also says, "Don't be afraid to get a babysitter. I had an aunt who was horrified that I had five babysitters' names on the refrigerator." Tucker says she politely ignored her aunt.

Some couples choose to take turns "maintaining primary responsibility," as environmentalist Frances Beinecke puts it. Beinecke says that when her husband took over at home, "I became much more engaged in the job."

As Beinecke says, "There are trade-offs to get to the top." So you may choose to hold off on your approach to the summit. Laura Tucker quit her job as a paid political staffer to be a volunteer political fundraiser and issue advocate when her second child was born. According to her, this choice led to her proudest political moment, ever: "I chaired the Planned Parenthood *Roe v. Wade* event when my kids were eight, ten, and twelve, and I spoke to one thousand people and talked about how my mother instilled in me this commitment to fight for equality. . . . It was so empowering, and my husband and my kids were sitting right there in front of me. My mom died a long time ago, so this was an opportunity to bring her into my life."

Lisa Madigan says that choosing to run for reelection as Illinois attorney general in 2010, instead of for governor or the US Senate, had to do with her children's ages. "Rebecca was three and Lucy one when I had to decide whether to run for higher office. My kids; they are just little; I need to be there for them. I usually get to go home at night. Not going home—that's not a sacrifice I was willing to make at the time," Madigan says.

Madigan continues, "It has to work in your personal world. If you've got conflict internally, listen to yourself as well as to others." Furthermore, she says, if you decide that you can't run for another office when others are asking you to, recognize that "if you just do your job, you're going to be fine. . . . If I do the job, these opportunities will be there in the future. People still think I can run for governor and win."

Understanding and supporting your partner's endeavors has its own rewards. After their children were grown, Currie says, "David started accepting teaching assignments out of the country," which gave him great pleasure. Currie points out, "Husbands aren't in the category of two-year-olds. You can negotiate with them."

Bordonaro says her husband "worked tirelessly" on her congressional campaign. Casagrande, who ran the student government at Penn State, says, "My husband was a senator in my student government, so he knew what he was getting into."

MacArthur Foundation executive Julia Stasch says her husband, Stan, a former university professor, "was where he wanted to be." She says, "He wanted a lot of autonomy over how he spent his time. I was looking to immerse myself. He does everything and I work."

Sometimes, you're winning but your partner is not. Pay attention and figure out how to make sure that you're not the only one enjoying the ride.

And sometimes you might need to take a break from politics. Maybe the family needs you to work at a job that pays better than your political one.

Myrna Lopez, a women's activist and public finance and economic development specialist, ran for reelection to the Richmond, California, city council and found the race tough and negative, and she lost. It was time to leave electoral politics. She says, "While I was on the city council, I had children. I want to create a positive environment for them." It was time to wait for a more positive political opportunity.

Gwen Page, whose full-time job as a school superintendent is very important to her, works hard to spend time with her children. She says, "I try to be mindful of the dream and that taking advantage of opportunities can be costly."

Molly Bordonaro said something similar: "I just try to be mindful of the possible. There is always an opportunity to have an impact, so don't ever feel that time slips away. I don't believe you get one shot, have one chapter. There's always an opportunity to have impact."

Sometimes, the trade-off is waiting for a campaign that is family friendly. Deanna Archuleta got her first opportunity when a city council seat opened up. At the time she was a "neighborhood mom" and PTA president advocating for safer street crossings, and friends suggested she run. One friend, a leader in the state legislator, went so far as to invite Archuleta to an EMILY's List fund-raising training session. But her then husband asked her not to run, and she declined. When a county commissioner seat opened up, Archuleta won and assumed responsibility for the jails, public hospital, and fire and sheriff's departments.

You don't stop being a woman when you choose to work in politics. Molly Bordonaro had an infant when she chaired George W. Bush's campaign in her region. "I was nursing in the campaign bus with four governors and our US senator watching."

Yes, there are trade-offs to get to the top for every political woman. Sometimes you'll make them because the timing's right. Sometimes you'll make them when the price isn't as high. But there are trade-offs for any person in any job. Politics may ask more of you than others; but the choices are yours, and you have every right to make them.

Strategic imperatives for having it all:

★ When others try to dissuade you from the decision you've made about your political future, even when they say it's to help you, pause, say thank you, and keep your own counsel. You won't regret taking the time to reflect.

★ Make sure you understand how your campaign will affect your family, and tell your family you appreciate their commitment to your dream.

★ Find aspects of your politicking that your family enjoys and focus on doing those things together as often as you can.

★ As you approach your own Election Day, seek the advice of the women in your community who hold or have held public office and ask them for advice on how they manage their marriages or families or sanity.

26

A local victory is a national one, too

In this age of instant, universal communication, you can make your local accomplishments visible on a much larger stage. To make your story resonate beyond your immediate environment, tell it nation-wide, highlighting its larger significance. Obviously, this is good practice if you seek federal office. But it's also good practice when you want the work you're doing locally to have national implications.

In either case, "I am everywhere" is the message you will keep sending. This message will make you a favorite for whatever Election Day is next, including the one you haven't quite decided on. The voters in whatever precinct you may be running in someday will know that you care about them and have fought on their behalf because you've focused on solving problems and addressing issues that span neighbor-hoods. Besides being the right thing to do, this strategy will engage you with more voters quickly. Election Day is all about this ground game, scrimmaging every day to get to the ending problems zone, as well as going door to door to get out the vote.

Lisa Madigan goes national by focusing her problem-solving agenda on consumer issues, safety issues, and family issues whose relevance reaches far beyond Illinois. Depending on what sort of remedy a problem needs, Madigan files a lawsuit, creates legislation, or uses her bully pulpit to bring attention to it. For instance, she testifies before Congress, joins or initiates national lawsuits, participates in problem-solving committees, lobbies national officials, and creates state model legislation. And, if her victories in Illinois have national implications, so does her performance of her job.

In 2009 Madigan filed a lawsuit against Wells Fargo charging that the bank had discriminated against African American and Latino borrowers. The Justice Department announced a settlement with Wells Fargo in 2012 that will compensate tens of thousands of those borrowers.

She developed the Illinois Sexual Assault Evidence Submission Act, now law in Illinois, which requires mandatory submission of rape kits for testing. She was part of the Justice Department team that negotiated a $25 billion settlement with the nation's five largest bank mortgage services over their robosigning practices.

Madigan recognizes that her commitment to causes that help people enables her to make both her local case to get elected and her national case that she's somebody to be reckoned with. Maybe, like Madigan, you don't know what your future holds. But you can still position yourself to be able to take advantage of a variety of options. Take on universal issues and broadcast your victories widely.

Like Madigan, you'll need to spell out specific proposals to merit national attention. General sentiments won't suffice. Even if some disagree with your ideas, you will have demonstrated intellect and ideas, and therefore your potential to be a credible national political figure. Campaigning or governing this way will also enable you to create ever more meaningful messages about your accomplishments, generate more and more substantial media coverage, and capture the attention of the opinion makers who shape Election Day futures.

Betsy Gotbaum, former public advocate for the city of New York, speaks proudly about reducing the paperwork associated with applying for food stamps from sixteen pages to four pages. She did this to help New Yorkers, but her remedy to benefit local residents had national importance, too. This is how you want to think.

When Barack Obama vacated his US Senate seat, many of Lisa Madigan's supporters wanted her to replace him. They thought a person who had so successfully demonstrated her understanding of and commitment to issues of national import deserved a next step into national office. Madigan disagreed, telling me, "I still have an ability as attorney general to have an impact on national issues."

Unlike Lisa Madigan, Cecilia Muñoz, director of the White House Domestic Policy Council, chose to leave Chicago for national office in Washington, DC. Muñoz was born in Detroit, where her parents had immigrated from Bolivia. After college, Muñoz moved to Chicago, where she worked on immigrants' rights. She then moved to Washington after being appointed senior vice president for the Office of Research, Advocacy, and Legislation at the National Council of La Raza. She told NPR's *Morning Edition*, "I guess outrage [over discrimination against Latinos] got me pretty far." Muñoz's career path—moving from local issue advocate to national issue advocate to the White House as director of the Domestic Policy Council—was made possible by her physical move from Chicago to DC. However, she was in the position to be offered the national position because her local work was promoted nationally.

Shelby Knox, who works for Change.org as director of organizing for women's rights, took advantage of national media exposure based on her local political advocacy and converted it into a national presence. Knox was fifteen when *The Education of Shelby Knox*, a film about her campaign for comprehensive sex education in the schools of Lubbock, Texas, was made, and she decided then to focus on the larger picture at the expense of the smaller, quitting the school swim team and choir. (Sex education again? Yep, this is our issue, like it or not. Knox says, "The choir director didn't like my having a film crew and being vocal around sex education.")

After the film was shown on PBS and at the Sundance Film Festival she began doing interviews and making public appearances all over the country. The Dixie Chicks even wrote a song about her.

Knox graduated from the University of Texas and landed in New York, and a few years later she was featured in an article in the Style section of the *New York Times* headlined "My Roommate, Gloria." Knox had been mentored by Gloria Steinem, who taught her how to build a national career as a feminist political activist.

We are not all cut out to become leaders of controversial national causes, nor lucky enough to team up with a celebrity like Gloria Steinem, nor prepared for the fast track to national attention. But nothing about Knox's ascension was a given.

Plenty of one-hit wonders are never heard from again. You have to keep stepping up to the plate and hitting the ball. Or recording new songs, or making new art. Resting on your laurels is not a strategy for winning Election Days.

All of these women have found ways to make significant change. Muñoz and Knox promoted themselves and their work so they could attain highly visible positions from which to operate. Maybe, you want that, too. Maybe, like Caroline Casagrande, you aspire to a national position like the United States Congress, but you're paying your dues in your state legislature. Or maybe, like Lisa Madigan, you want to do local work that has national implications. Whether you are a PTA president, a city council member, or a state legislator, you can make your local victories national, too. Here is how:

- Help national leadership be recognized in your community, and then ask them to return the favor.

- Create model legislation and get it passed. Share that good news.

- Implement model executive or administrative policies, for instance an office flex-time policy. Share that good news.

- Volunteer to work on national projects and make substantive contributions to them. Publicize those contributions in national media.

- Ask your member of Congress to invite you to testify. Publicize that testimony.

- Advocate for the agendas of organizations that share your public policy goals. Publicize that advocacy.

- Build and lead organizations of like-minded women officials, and take responsibility for publicizing their work.

- Hold your organization's meetings around the country, so you can publicize your work in regional media markets outside your home base.

- Participate in national women's issues conferences, at meetings of women donors, and at gatherings of public officials who are developing strategies to advance women candidates. Publicize this participation.

Strategic imperatives for making your local action count in every corner:

★ Refine your local message so that it is universally applicable.

★ Don't forget to dance with the one who brung you as you leave the old neighborhood.

★ When you have friends in high places, invite them to all your old neighborhoods. You'll give your new friends a glimpse into your character and demonstrate that you have supporters all over the place.

★ Longtime Speaker of the US House of Representatives Tip O'Neill was right when he coined the phrase "All politics is local," a useful concept for the political woman in the age of social media, when international distribution of your every local word is just a click away. You can be an international and a local sensation at the same time.

---| PART IV |---

CONFRONT, CO-OPT, CONTROL

27

Learn to negotiate

esearch on women as public officials concludes that women in public-policy-making roles are better at collaborating and building consensus than their male counterparts. Yet these women office holders wouldn't be making policy if they weren't intensely competitive and willing to deploy campaign tactics that are the antithesis of collaborative. Consequently, the most successful among them demonstrate two important qualities: an ability to put differences aside in order to negotiate a beneficial compromise, and an ability to resist compromise if that's what it takes to win.

Women win elections using the same aggressive tactics men do. But once you win you have to govern, and negotiation and compromise is how governments reach decisions. Caroline Casagrande says, "We [Democrats and Republicans] have to work together." She says this collaboration "has led to a lot of thoughtful policies, the kinds of reforms that would have been very hard for just one party to push through. These big ideas, these big concepts, need both sides. Otherwise, it's nuclear war." As Sharon Broome points out, "There is always another issue. You don't want disagreement to be a barrier to the relationship." This is where becoming a skilled and forceful negotiator comes in.

Implied in the willingness to negotiate is this notion about that other guy: His issues are your issues. His agenda is your agenda. His worries are your worries. If you take control, you control your destiny: you're able to move the agenda and negotiate deals that work for him and for you.

Lori Healey is my role model in this department. Healey completed graduate school in her early twenties, receiving a master's degree in public administration, and has held successively bigger jobs in state and local governments. Even so, she says, "I'm still routinely the only woman in the room," making the negotiation that much more challenging. She was also a founding member of Illinois Executive Women in State Government, demonstrating her commitment to changing the negotiating dynamics.

My mother, Mary Robinson Sive, was an elected school board member in my hometown, and, as far as she knows, the first woman president of the school board. When she discussed her public service with me, she said, "You have to deal with the situation as it is, not as how you would like it to be. I can't say it bothered me. I had to deal with it." She negotiated as best she could to yield the best results for Pearl River families.

Lori Healey took the same tack negotiating on behalf of Chicago families. Deal with the situation facing you and learn to negotiate so that you achieve the best outcome. Today, Healey sums up her career this way: "I'm about the deal."

Healey hastens to add that you have to be prepared for the deal to work. When Healey was Chicago mayor Richard M. Daley's chief of staff, she spent a lot of time negotiating with members of the city council. As she ticked off some of the tough issues a mayor and city council have to address, such as neighborhood economic development plans and the allocation of police officers and firefighters, she says, "Having to deal with a legislative body is always a compromise so you can meet everybody's needs. For the most part, anytime you can reach a compromise, that's a good thing, a definition of good public policy."

However, Healey is no pushover. "Sometimes, you just have to not back down. You just have to be able to stand your ground," Healey says. It's possible you've already made some compromises. If you compromise further, you will diminish the return on your policy position, which you are confident is the right one. Equally unfortunately, you will diminish your ability to be in the lead in the future, because you've probably already said, "That's it."

"I would stand up and say, 'Discussion over,' and walk out of the room," Healey says, admitting she has done this from time to time. I say, sometimes you just have to be disruptive to make your point. Healey was a debater in high school. That experience holds her in good stead. "I kicked ass at debate my whole life." Now there's a plan.

Healey says, "I don't care so much about being liked. I just want to be respected." That's rule one. That helps.

If it feels like you're about to become a yes person, don't compromise and negotiate any further. Yes people don't run things, or if they do, it's not for long. Healey says that when a staff person proposed a "yes people" solution, she would say, "No, that's stupid." Someone once said to me, "Easy gets you nothing." If a proposed compromise feels like the easiest thing to do because backing down feels a whole lot more comfortable than reasserting your position, don't do it. You'll have little to show at the back end.

You may find yourself being asked to negotiate away something that might seem like a small policy matter to others, but that to you is nonnegotiable. Your best move is to tell your opponent that. Honesty will work better than a negotiation that doesn't seem honest. Small policy matters can become big rhetorical ones. Be clear up front about what compromises you can and can't make. In this context, Healey points out, "There may come a time when there is another issue. . . . Having a positive disagreement is the basis for future agreements where there is mutual respect." She says, "Taking the time to get to know someone, develop a personal relationship, even if you disagree on policy," is very valuable. This will put you on good footing when you come back to the negotiating table.

In this context, the arc of Healey's career is instructive. The first phase was to conquer the material. The second was to develop the self-confidence necessary for success. "Make yourself give speeches. Be active in meetings. Be noticed." Having a sense of humor also helps. "It's important," Healey says.

However, it's equally important to recognize when you've gotten the best deal you can and that to press more will just send you downhill. Live to fight another day and maintain position are your rules of thumb here. If this sounds depressing, take heart from these words of advice shared in an *Elle* magazine story about ten powerful Washington, DC, women, which included young Republican powerhouse Jennifer Hing, communications director of the House Appropriations Committee: "The solutions always require compromise," she says. "It's what the founders intended."

Stephanie Cutter, adviser to President Obama and First Lady Michelle Obama, and Mary Matalin, adviser to presidents Bush and Reagan, are masters at executing uncompromising political strategies in order to win elections. Matalin's mentor was Lee Atwater, the senior political strategist for President George H. W. Bush in his successful 1988 campaign. Cutter's was US senator Ted Kennedy, who in turn was schooled by his own dynastic family. Healey summarizes this approach this way: "Be smart enough to grab what you can."

Healey says, "I know how to throw a punch." Cutter told *Marie Claire* magazine the same thing, "I know how to throw a punch." A colleague was quoted in the same article, saying, "She's a bulldozer when she needs to be." When Cutter was profiled in the *New York Times*, a colleague said of her, "She is an old-school, take-no-prisoners political operative. Losing is not tolerated." Part of this take-no-prisoners approach is negotiation when it's necessary to create the best operational plan. One example is in presidential debates, where extensive negotiations result in a signed memo of understanding between the candidates.

In these situations, Healey says, "Just go for it. Don't second-guess yourself."

Cutter, Matalin, Healey, and the women coming up behind them also develop opportunities for their bosses to talk about issues in ways that create the perception that the view expressed is universal and they're in charge of this universal agenda item. The strategy is to minimize the number of times tough negotiations are needed or a mixed message is promulgated. For instance, in the 2012 presidential election, improving the American economy was typically discussed as a matter of helping "middle class" families. A July 2012 CNN headline summed up: "Obama, Romney fight for middle class voters." That gets votes. While naysayers bemoan lack of specificity, these political women know better. It's the specifics that give rise to disagreement and disaffection. Instead, these women always seek to make sure their candidate's issues are the voters' issues so no apparent compromise is required. This is complicated when there are significant differences of policy that become evident over the course of a campaign. Once you win, you can negotiate the details of your policy proposals.

Debbie Walsh, director of the Center for American Women and Politics at Rutgers University, says, "Women are more likely to work across the aisle and find compromise." In the same article from *The Hill*, entitled "Elect More Women to End Gridlock," author Anne Kim writes, "Female senators have a markedly more bipartisan vote record than their male peers do." I have heard US senator Patty Murray make this point as part of the rationale for electing more women to the US senate. According to the *New York Times*, the "female senators have a quarterly bipartisan dinner." The *Times* said, "Ms. Gillibrand said she recently found herself sitting next to Senator Susan Collins, Republican of Maine, during the nasty fiscal fight seizing Congress. 'She touched my arm and said, "Kirsten, if you and I were negotiating the budget we would have gotten it done a week ago."'" Maybe that would have happened; maybe it wouldn't have, but belief in the power of negotiating to do good is key to its success.

US senator Mary Landrieu makes this strategy work for her by developing legislative proposals that so clearly benefit her constituents that the legislative sausage making (read: negotiation and compromise) required to develop and pass them gets put aside. Therefore, the hard feelings that can emanate from protracted negotiation are not apparent to all but the most policy-wonkish constituents. Here is how she put it in her press release about passage of the Restore Act: "The RESTORE Act, which was introduced by Sen. Landrieu . . . will dedicate 80 percent of BP penalties paid under the Clean Water Act to the Gulf states for ecological and economic restoration." Passage of the Restore Act was called a "giant step forward for the health of the Gulf [of Mexico]" by the Gulf Restoration Network, a group of serious policy wonks that has disagreed with Senator Landrieu on other occasions. This agenda is not postpartisan, but it is bipartisan. It feels like it's everybody's.

If you're running for office, the plain and simple arithmetic is that you need more voters than the other girl. If you're seeking ever-higher appointive office, competition will be increasingly stiff, and the decision makers will have more at stake. Make sure any compromise you make along the way will work for your long-term agenda.

Landrieu says that her office handles approximately five thousand requests for help each year. Part of the responsibility of a US senator, these requests—from veterans, students, or families in need—are handled without regard to political affiliation. Constituents frequently come up to Landrieu and thank her, saying, "I don't agree with you on all your issues, but you sure helped me with my problem." Sometimes, they even tell her, "I'm a Republican, but you helped me [anyway]." She hears, "I don't agree with Senator Landrieu all the time, but I do agree most of the time." When it comes to Election Day, these voters' sentiments matter.

"Even presidents do constituent service," Landrieu says. That's because it's a duty, but also because constituent service is a way of demonstrating shared concerns. As Landrieu says, these shared concerns can go a long way toward overcoming political differences. Your goal is to find shared concerns and address them to help build trust. That way when an issue does come up, you can work together on a solution based on that past relationship.

Strategic imperatives for handling negotiating from a position of strength:

★ When you know you've got the right approach to a policy issue, don't compromise yourself or that approach as you work yourself back from a negotiating loss. Politely but firmly maintain your position.

★ When the issue positions are thorny and the discussion gets heated, remember that every family issue—and that's pretty much any issue—is a women's issue, too. If the circumstances call for it, return rhetorically to the notion of sisterhood as a way to bring people back together.

★ The notion of "good cop, bad cop" is useful when you're negotiating and seeking to control the agenda. Figure out which you want to be in each instance.

★ Say you're willing to be the "bad cop" when negotiating as part of a team and you want to demonstrate you're willing to go the extra mile without regard to your own best interest. Most people will give up that one in a hurry. If the team wins, you'll look like a real hero.

28

Men will accept it when you take charge, even though they say they won't

On your way toward Election Day, you'll become an expert at negotiating compromises even while assuming authority and responsibility, until no one wants anyone but you to do the job you want. This willingness to do more than your share while killing them with kindness is an unbeatable combination.

In 1992, Ilana D. Rovner became the first woman ever appointed to the United States Court of Appeals for the Seventh Circuit. She was only the twenty-sixth woman appointed to any federal court of appeals. Only 14 percent of federal appeals court judges were women at that time. In 2012, it was 31 percent.

Rovner did plenty of grinding work to earn her appointment, but she says she used an additional technique to make the men in charge give her what she wanted. Rovner says her "kindness" is a professional as well as a personal commitment. Rovner grew up in Philadelphia, after emigrating from Latvia, the only girl child in her extended family to survive the Holocaust. She says that she always felt she had to do something important with her life to justify her survival, and what better contribution to society for one who had survived terror than to devote herself to kind leadership in manner and in deed?

"I love the 'broken wings,'" says Rovner. "I wanted to help the broken wings. I wanted to change the world. I wanted to make it a better place."

She went to Bryn Mawr College and began law school at Georgetown University but left to get married; she finished up in 1966 at Chicago-Kent. In 1973 she joined the US attorney's Chicago office, where she was eventually promoted to chief of the public protection unit, the first woman supervisor in the office. "I was willing to do the most unpopular cases," Rovner says. "I worked my heart out. I would take anything, things the men eschewed."

When her boss, then US attorney James "Big Jim" R. Thompson, became the governor of Illinois he appointed her, in 1977, to the post of deputy governor and legal counsel. I met her not long after that while leading the campaign, mentioned previously, to convince Thompson to appoint a women's issues adviser to his senior staff.

When a federal district court judgeship opened up, Rovner said she wanted it, and Thompson and others supported her campaign for it. Ronald Reagan appointed her to the post in 1984. A few years after that, the boys in charge lobbied for her again when she asked for a US court of appeals appointment, and then president George H. W. Bush swore her in in 1992.

You might look at Rovner's career trajectory and consider her lucky. After all, it was lucky that her boss became a governor who knew presidents. But if Rovner is lucky, that's the sort of luck that only comes to a certain kind of woman: a woman who puts in the time working to make herself indispensable to the men in charge.

By the time Rovner sought a federal judgeship, she had spent years solving other people's problems. Yet, she says, she always made it clear she was grateful for the opportunity to help. Rovner said to me, "It's a way of nurturing a relationship and letting people know that you're there to be a resource. Anywhere you are included, you really want to say: I enjoyed working on that. I'm very appreciative of your including me."

Letitia Baldrige, Jackie Kennedy's social secretary, has it right: you can't say thank you too often. Receiving gratitude is the greatest validation most people will ever experience. At every opportunity in every circumstance, say thank you. (There are seventy-six different examples of thank-yous in *Letitia Baldrige's New Manners for New Times: A Complete Guide to Etiquette*). And thanking people will inspire gratitude in response.

After a while, you'll have the pocketbook full of IOUs you'll need to win on Election Day.

Mary Kay Henry is another example of a woman with a generous spirit who made a gradual ascent, employing dedication and hard work: she was the first woman to be elected international president of the Service Employees International Union (SEIU), which is the fastest-growing American union, with more than two million members, in part because of the growth of women members, including nurses and nursing home, child care, and home health-care workers. Henry started as a local organizer in California. Seventeen years later, she was elected to the SEIU's international executive board. Eight years after that she was appointed an international executive vice president, and in 2010 she was unanimously elected president by its executive board.

Henry climbed steadily up her institutional ladder, finally gaining the top rung, which had previously only been occupied by men. This experience is common for women who reach the top of large and complex organizations. You may do the same, but if you have the opportunity to step up the pace, make sure you take it.

Strategic imperatives for leading men:

★ Be firm but kind. A little bit of sugar does help the medicine go down.

★ Step up to the front and be sure you're visible when you take charge and deliver.

★ Encourage people to keep watching as you keep getting their jobs done.

★ Make it clear you want the next big assignment, the one that will likely involve a lot of men working for you. Make it clear you want it bad.

★ Be kind to everyone, no matter how unpleasant they are to you, because you never know how the relationship might benefit you or whether that person may be your opponent on Election Day.

★ Remember that power is an aphrodisiac. You don't want to play with fire, but you do want to use that vibe to your advantage.

29

Communications: a breakdown

Money in the bank and a network of powerful friends won't mean anything if you don't establish yourself in the minds of voters before Election Day. If you've done something great for your constituents and they don't know you took that leadership role, they won't know to turn to you in the future. Likewise, if you mess up and run for cover instead of explaining your mistake, you'll miss an opportunity to generate the support of your constituents. Of course, you'll always work diligently to meet the specs for the job you have or the one you seek, but unless your efforts are visible, what good will that do you as you dream of your big Election Day? That's where using the media comes in.

As you plan your communications strategies, think presidential inauguration, royal wedding, World Series, blockbuster movie, celebrity tell-all, or comeback tour: you're aware of them, and you probably even have an opinion about all of them, even if you didn't watch the broadcasts or go to the movie or read the book or attend the concert. That's because pop culture is in the ether. That means it's free and available for you to use however you can to heighten your presence and advance your campaign. Don't diminish serious subjects or patriotic moments with pop culture references, but do use them to capture the public's attention when the opportunity presents.

One goal is to build your personal visibility, using pop culture images and messages, especially those that portray women positively and powerfully. For instance, in presentation and causes you champion, emulate Reese Witherspoon, not Kim Kardashian; Meryl Streep, not Betty White; Beyoncé, not Madonna. Don't get me wrong here; I have a lot of admiration for all of these women, who have chutzpah to burn. But, in the political context, women voters want women with chutzpah who help other women lead better lives and don't send mixed messages about personal behavior. These celebrities are role models for you as you become better known and build a following.

Instead of bemoaning the meaninglessness of pop culture "news," get with the program and make it work for you. Consider: During the 2012 UN meetings in New York, President Obama found time to chat with the ladies of *The View. New York Times* columnist Frank Bruni wrote "Pop Goes the President" about the focus of both presidential candidates on pop culture imagery, asserting, "This presidential election will go down as the one in which the pop-culture pander reached its ludicrous apotheosis." Bruni mentioned Governor Romney's "swoon for Snooki." 'Nuff said.

The Avon cosmetics tagline, "The company for women," is a great example of savvy marketing. It sends an expansive, positive message while remaining connected to the purpose of the products: makeup for women. Think of promoting yourself in a similarly broad context.

During National Breast Cancer Awareness Month in October 2012, there was a presidential debate covering domestic policy issues. Both Michelle Obama and Ann Romney showed up in hot pink to show support for breast cancer survivors and research. Later, on the campaign trail, President Obama was spotted wearing a pink bracelet signaling the same. It doesn't hurt your image to connect yourself to the spirit (and look) of the moment.

The same month, "You Don't Own Me," a big pop hit for Lesley Gore in 1964, was reworked for a public service announcement encouraging women to vote. The ad, which went viral, featured girls and women of all backgrounds singing their hearts out along with the original, interspersed with just a few taglines: "Your vote is your voice," "When women vote women win," and "Get your rosaries off my ovaries."

Social media content like this works brilliantly because it's inclusive and fast. You will want to use it systematically and comprehensively. This focus means you are not obsessing over the number of times your name appears in the local newspaper (23 percent of Americans read a daily newspaper), but instead making sure people see you in cyberspace.

It isn't that those newspaper and TV photo-ops at the opening of the local food pantry (where you volunteer) or child care center (that your children attend) or hospital wing (that one of your donors funded) are not important. They still are. But they are more important when you repurpose them on social media outlets to expand your reach.

Remember this advice from Caroline Casagrande: "Just go and do the right thing. People see through parsed words and lack of candor." Social media is much harder to control than old-fashioned news. Remember Mitt Romney's "47 percent" comment? Your best option is to be clear and to the point and only say what your mother would be comfortable reading you said on the front page of that local newspaper (sage advice from one of my political mentors). And if you feel you can't be transparent and direct, don't say anything at all.

While you're shaping your message, try to deliver it in the largest rhetorical context you can. This is particularly important when you're discussing tough or touchy issues. In 2012, when access to abortion became a hot-button issue, pro-choice activists recast their message as the right to manage one's own reproductive health, not to obtain an abortion. Then they connected reproductive health to economic security. Voters responded positively. Proof was in the gender gap in women voters' preference for President Obama over Governor Romney. Women favored President Obama because he expressly said he believed that women's reproductive health decisions should be theirs, not the government's, and he would deliver for women because he believes this. Cecile Richards backed him up every chance she got, becoming a constant presence on TV, even taking a leave from Planned Parenthood to act as a surrogate for him during the presidential campaign.

Maria Shriver, former TV news reporter and First Lady of California, presents herself across all kinds of media as politically serious but friendly and approachable. When she was First Lady, she hosted an annual conference at which other First Ladies conversed about political issues affecting women's lives in a comfortable setting in front of a large audience. Now, she hosts a website that also feels comfortable, and tweets personalized messages about her family life that also make larger points about issues that concern her. For instance, she tweeted a picture of her son and his cousin at an event for a disability charity her brother founded.

Melissa Harris-Perry and Shelby Knox, well-known expert communicators on women's issues, use pop culture and social media to enlarge their presence, image, and political influence. Each is now well positioned to win a big Election Day and every primary along the way.

Melissa Harris-Perry is the only tenured professor in the United States to host her own political-issues television show. The Twitter hashtag for her eponymous MSNBC show is "#nerdland." According to *The Oxford English Dictionary*, a nerd is "boringly studious." That would describe a lot of university professors. But it wouldn't describe Harris-Perry or, of course, celebrity TV hosts in general.

With #nerdland, Harris-Perry is claiming the new-media space for studious lovers of politics and public policy, promoting the proposition that caring about public policy can be cool. That makes her and her point of view cool, too—pure genius, if you're seeking to build a significant and influential political presence, as Harris-Perry surely is.

Harris-Perry reinforces her cool factor via her personal appearance. Viewers know who made her earrings and how long it takes for her to get her hair done. Jan Schakowsky admired her shoes one day. After sharing personal points like these, Harris-Perry returns to a serious political matter. Viewers have been drawn in by her personality and her sharing these enticing tidbits and become interested in her perspective on serious political topics. It's brilliant, really.

Harris-Perry's Twitter followers learned about her family's Mardi Gras barbecue, that she jogs only to the tunes of female hip-hop singers, that she is an interpretive dancer, and that she loves Red Lobster cheesy biscuits. They've also seen pictures of her at the Easter Egg Roll on the South Lawn of the White House (the day after she wore an Easter bonnet on her TV show). And that on top of everything else that connects her to the zeitgeist, she's revealed that, like President Obama, she's the child of a white mother and a black father, and that her mom was born a Mormon, which gave her special insight into 2012 presidential candidate Mitt Romney.

She also revealed on Twitter that she had a life-saving abortion. The message that time was that though she may be president of #nerdland, she makes difficult life choices just like everyone else.

Harris-Perry began to take this approach in her first book, *Barbershops, Bibles, and BET: Everyday Talk and Black Political Thought*, which already sounds like a lot more fun than most professors' doctoral theses. Her second book, *Sister Citizen: Shame, Stereotypes, and Black Women in America*, had the same provocative pop appeal.

Harris-Perry may have her own TV show, but most of her promotional strategies are free, and they are as readily available to you as they are to her. You, too, can write about your personal life, placing it in a larger political context that connects to the campaign you're running. You, too, can share pictures on Twitter that evoke positive shared experiences or your special qualities or interests.

Teenage reproductive rights activist turned grown-up activist Shelby Knox tweets all the time on all manner of women-related topics. She shared her Twitter and other social media tips with me:

- Set up accounts on different social media platforms and cross-post to your Twitter feed.

- Tweet relentlessly about every issue you care about (even if you only care a little).

- Use the tweets to establish a personal connection to the issues.

- Use Twitter to connect with other people, especially if you're geographically or socially isolated (as Knox says she was as a teenager in Lubbock).

- Tweet about the people you've met, what they care about, and why their concerns are your concerns.

- Share on Twitter stories about yourself that connect to others' experiences, even if those others are celebrities.

- If you meet someone famous, tweet the news. (Forget what your mother told you about not showing off.)

- Join organizations that are in "the sphere you want to influence." And then communicate about them digitally from an insider's vantage point.

- Live tweet from events. Get on every social media platform with your own name and interact with the influencers. (Friend important people on Facebook and invite them to your Google circle.)

- Share personal information frequently.

- Create online petitions and publicize them in social media. In 2012, Knox was the guide for three young students from Montclair, New Jersey, when they posted a petition on Change.org because they discovered in civics class that a woman hadn't moderated a US general election presidential debate since 1992. One of the girls says, "It was actually pretty amazing how it happened. We wrote the petition, put it on . . . and it gained 100,000 signatures with no press support. Then the petition became a media sensation." There is a sisterhood. Use it to promote yourself and your causes.

As director of the Jane Addams Hull-House Museum, Lisa Lee specialized in tying serious political topics to pop culture in an institutional context. For decades, the Jane Addams Hull-House Museum, located on the campus of the University of Illinois at Chicago, was a typical old museum with period furnishings and unenticing exhibits. The museum's subject is, of course, Jane Addams, the human rights crusader who developed new strategies for addressing municipal problems that still plague Chicago and other cities and bedevil public officials. Over the last decade, Lee transformed it into her own version of #nerdland. She addressed Addams's concerns and the museum's mission in exhibits and events using hip and appealing language and images and then promoted them liberally in digital media. One recent exhibit focused on a notorious Chicago gang to encourage discussion of their nonviolent community service work.

Lee, who has since moved on to another job at the university, also took on provocative personal topics with public policy implications. SEX+++, a series of "radically inclusive documentary films about positive sexuality," offered a space for discussions of sex, culture, and pleasure. At Lee's Jane Addams events, scholars, poets, writers, musicians, actors, and artists gathered to talk about racial discrimination, gender inequality, sexual freedom, education, and local and organic food. Her institution became part of the message, just as you can use your own personality and media smarts and organizational context to become part of the message you want to convey.

Here are some more tactics to make modern media contact:

- Volunteer for any and all radio and TV appearances. That link can go worldwide.
- Upload those links to your websites and all your social media accounts.
- Share those links with all of your contact lists through e-mail and digital newsletters.
- Post your newsletters, links, and pages to other sites.
- Post video of your speeches or ads or event coverage on YouTube.
- Use YouTube as a resource to learn about your competition.
- Become a constant presence at local events like church bazaars, parades, community festivals, and farmers' markets. Circulate and make friends.
- Use innovative tactics and media to advance your message: theater, film, book clubs, and protests.
- Never giggle—that's a sure sign of lack of confidence.

- And always speak in a fairly low tone of voice. That sounds more authoritative. There is still too much sexist media out there to give them an opening.

Here are a few more from activist Rachel Durchslag:

- "Learn how to be digestible. You can't scare people into caring."

- "Great lobbyists don't try to get the people who are all the way to NO." They find the people who agree, and sign them up. That's what great candidates do, too.

- "Talk every day" with your media and communications staff and make a plan for that day, in the context of that day's events. Connect the dots from your message to those events.

And here are my recommendations for media relations when you're building your own image while staffing someone else's campaign, whether as a paid employee or as a friend.

- Be the spokesperson.

- Develop and constantly update your personal media contact list in a digital database that allows you to create multiple lists without duplicating contacts. Use this list each time you have a story to tell.

- Volunteer to contact the press when there is a story to tell, no matter how small. Repeated contact results in familiarity, which breeds not contempt but dependence.

- Represent your campaign or organization in meetings—the local ones, and for sure the regional and national ones—where candidates, staffers, and advocates are gathered. Then spread the word about your own commitment to the cause (as well as your candidate's).

- Advocate for coverage of your activities in institutional newsletters and press announcements.

- Create a media list and make sure everyone on it is contacted when you are invited to speak, in order to make sure your speech is well covered.

- Create all-embracing messages for your activities, however narrowly or locally focused the event may appear at first blush, and use them in all communications about yourself.

There is no shortage of ways to get your message out. The goal is to do so in ways that are easy for your prospective endorsers and voters to access, to connect the message to pop culture or zeitgeist topics and personalities they care about, and to present yourself as understanding the most modern modes of communication. If you eventually become a candidate whose campaign requires professional staff, you can determine with your staff how to allocate the communications tasks. If your campaign staff is all volunteer, these duties can still be shared, because you're all still working, albeit without pay. Perhaps one day you'll have money for paid media, and will of course always portray yourself as a caring and approachable person, the best way to win voters' hearts. Meanwhile, access the world with free media.

Strategic imperatives for using media to your advantage:

★ Use the most modern and hippest forms of communicating.

★ Talk about serious issues with unlikely people and in unlikely but attractive settings.

★ Identify trending pop culture topics and connect your policy positions and public programs to those topics.

★ Ask artists, musicians, dancers, poets, and actors to speak out on your issues. Also ask them to create media about you and your campaign.

★ Connect issues that, on the surface, don't appear connected in a way that really makes an impact (for example, make the connection between food policy and hunger by having a poet read her poems, as Lisa Lee did).

★ While you connect every message of yours to your overall substantive campaign theme, capture that message in a pop culture phrase or concept, such as "Forward" in the 2012 Obama campaign, which echoes Nike's "Just Do It." If you can recruit a celebrity (in your community), have that celebrity transmit the message for you. It will connect you to those who aren't otherwise paying attention.

★ Remember, however, there is nothing like the personal touch: sometimes even those running for the highest offices or those supporting them send their own tweets. (See Michelle Obama's Twitter handle @FLOTUS; her personal tweets contain the signature "mo.")

30

Negative media, damage control, and dressing for the part

Fair warning: This is the chapter that may remind you of junior high—that time you heard catty remarks about you or your girl-friends or imagined you did. Of the time you first thought, Why is the world such a horrible place sometimes? Or thought later, when you were feeling more positive, How can I fix this? This isn't right, and it's not fair.

Negativity is like a weed: it just keeps sprouting. You can't wish it away; all you can do is keep weeding. And you're not alone. No woman seeking power will escape negative attention. It's inevitable. It just is.

When Hillary Clinton was First Lady she was called on to account for her involvement in a questionable family investment. She held a press conference to answer questions from the media, wearing an image-softening pink sweater. The strategy was a common one: using your appearance to reinforce your message. This is a calculation people in public life make every day. The events Clinton spoke about that day set her and her husband back, but Clinton came back roaring. She is admired unilaterally, and is roaring still. You can do the same, if you're ever thinking the day calls for that pink sweater.

Carol Bellamy refers to politics as "a fishbowl." Molly Bordonaro says, "I recognized anyone can say anything about me—this is politics." Gwen Page is blunt, too: "It is so arduous and you get criticized all of the time." Bottom line, she says, "Keep your nose clean. Make sure you are aboveboard. There are no secrets. Anything you say or write, expect it to be on a billboard at any time. Watch your acquaintances. There can be guilt by association."

Political women experience all kinds of negative attention of billboard dimensions: you didn't earn it; you don't deserve it; you made the wrong decision or took the wrong position; you switched your policy without explanation, and to an even worse position; you're a weasel; your partner's a schmuck; he or she is messing with someone else's partner; your family's a bunch of losers; your friends are criminals; you're a boozer; you have loose morals; you should be in jail.

This will happen. But everyone makes mistakes, and the public knows that just as well as you do. No one expects you to be Mother Teresa. Even Mother Teresa wasn't Mother Teresa, if taking money from dictators is a sin. And people love a sinner who redeems herself by battling for the welfare of others. Scandal sells, but what voters really want is officials who work hard on their behalf, and that's about it.

Nevertheless, be prepared: Attacks can happen anytime and anywhere. Have a plan ready to put into action anytime, anywhere.

The most basic element of a crisis management plan is to respond quickly, in your own words, stating the truth and explaining why you are still the best person for the job. Occasionally, the best response is no response.

Once, when chancery clerk Monica Banks's staff recommended she respond publicly to a charge that race had been a determinant of her political endorsements, Banks told them no. "It was important to me that I not let anyone turn my campaign into a racial campaign. I did not run on color. I ran on capability and competence to do the job I was seeking. My campaign slogan was and still is 'The People's Chancery Clerk.' I just didn't address it. Nothing I felt I had to publicly address."

Banks says, "Pick your battles wisely. Every battle that hits the front line is not one you have to be a part of."

Her plan was to keep doing such a good job that the negativity would fade over time. And it has: while she won her first race by twenty-three votes, she was unopposed in her last race.

Because Banks is a religious person, she also says, "You have to know when to let the Lord fight a battle for you." As you might imagine, I recommend a slightly more active approach.

Former Louisiana Supreme Court Chief Justice Kimball says, "I used to always tell the press we can talk about whatever you want—on the record or off, but if it's on the record, I need a few minutes to think about how I want to say this."

Gwen Page says, "It's part of human nature to have detractors. But, if it's a real problem, I deal with it. You have to keep your vision in front of you. You have to have hope and faith in 'the system.'"

Deanna Archuleta was troubled when a reporter wanted to write about her divorce instead of about her campaign. Based on that experience, she says, "You face it; you say it will be a story for a couple days." She directed her communications staffer to say to the reporter, "Would you want someone writing about your divorce? What makes you think Deanna would?" That won't always work, but in this case the reporter rethought the story and focused elsewhere.

When Barbara Flynn Currie sponsored a bill lifting the limits on campaign contributions if an independent entity spends above a certain amount, she was criticized by campaign finance reformers and in the media. But the weight of the evidence of her reformer credentials is on Currie's side. That's where you want to be, too, if you take a position that may alienate some of your core constituents. Currie says, "I have an extremely tough skin." That helps, too.

And it's virtually a given that you'll run into some plain old sexism on your way to the election. In 2012, when Mia Love was running for a seat in Congress, the *Daily Mail* called her a "fitness instructor," forgetting to mention that she was a sitting mayor. The best advice for how to handle such incidents is embodied in the name of the nonpartisan project Name It. Change It., which monitors the media for sexism and publicizes this bad behavior. When you do, you will find a sympathetic audience: most people have realized that sexist remarks have no place in the political discourse.

On the other hand, there may come a time when charges being leveled at you require a shout back.

California attorney general Kamala Harris had a relationship with Willie Brown, who had long been separated from his wife, in 1994 just before he ran for reelection as the mayor of San Francisco. In 2003, the affair was discussed when she made her first run for public office, for district attorney of San Francisco County, and she was accused of having an inescapable conflict of interest. When a reporter from *San Francisco Weekly* asked if she'd be able to prosecute the mayor if his administration were accused of wrongdoing, she said, "If there is corruption, it will be prosecuted. It's a no-brainer, but let's please move on."

Harris also told the reporter: "His career is over; I will be alive and kicking for the next forty years. I do not owe him a thing."

The same writer called her "whip-smart, hard-working, and well-credentialed to be San Francisco's top prosecutor." That's what the county's voters thought, too, and she won her race for DA. And that's what the state's voters saw a few years later when Harris was elected attorney general for the state of California. And that must be what President Obama considered when he named her a cochair of his 2012 reelection campaign.

Standing up to detractors requires self-confidence and a belief in your power to do good. You probably wouldn't be seeking a political career if you didn't already have these qualities, but Harris's accomplishment is impressive nonetheless. Remember it when the time comes: address your naysayer head-on and remind those who would judge you just how gifted you really are.

That's the right approach, and it worked for Harris. Now US senator, then Harvard law professor Elizabeth Warren, offers another scenario, one you won't want to emulate. In the spring of 2012, while Warren was campaigning for the Senate, it was revealed that she had identified herself in law school directories in the 1980s and 1990s as Native American, possibly benefiting from universities' attempts to diversify their faculties. It took Warren five weeks after the story broke to fully acknowledge it.

"At some point after I was hired by them, I . . . provided that information to the University of Pennsylvania and Harvard," she said in a statement to the *Boston Globe*. "My Native American heritage is part of who I am, I'm proud of it and I have been open about it."

She wasn't exactly shouting, and she didn't explain why she'd never mentioned her heritage as a candidate. Instead, at one point during those five weeks, Warren told the *Boston Herald*, "I listed myself in the directory in the hopes that it might mean that I would be invited to a luncheon, a group something that might happen with people who are like I am. Nothing like that ever happened, that was clearly not the use for it and so I stopped checking it off." For me, this response was unbearably painful. It was the proverbial nails on a blackboard.

Five months later, Warren was forced to run a campaign ad addressing this subject. In that ad, Warren says, "As a kid I never asked my mom for documentation when she talked about her Native American heritage. What kid would?" This ad was discussed in an article entitled "Elizabeth Warren's Family History May Be a Lie. Have You Checked Yours?"

This is really good advice. I've recommended already that you learn as much as you can about your own life and your family members' lives. Big campaigns spend thousands doing "opposition research" so that every flaw or failing in the opposition can be trumpeted. But no matter how modest the office you're seeking, doing this research will be a good use of your time. You want to know what's out there so that you can determine how to deal with it and so it doesn't distract you or force you to spend scarce resources.

If you're caught out, even through no fault of your own, shout back and make your case. Forget trying to be a saint. Justice Kimball put it plainly when I asked her what she would advise a candidate who is flawed: "It depends on how flawed." Anyway, she said, "Handle it up front."

When Susan G. Komen for the Cure withdrew funding for Planned Parenthood, saying that it couldn't support organizations under investigation, the outcry almost destroyed the foundation. It diminished the brand and the agency's credibility almost beyond recognition. That is because the reason for Komen's decision actually appeared to be a political disagreement with Planned Parenthood. To add insult to injury, the Komen disaster rolled out for hours on the Internet before Komen issued any response. In a follow-up piece by Virgil Scudder, the Public Relations Society of America's newsletter advised:

> Listen to your professional staff, especially the PR team. If you think they are wrong, bring in outside counsel for a second opinion.
> Be aware of the timing of what you do. This snafu came in the middle of a political season in which abortion was a hot issue.
> Weigh the power and impact of social media before you act.
> Avoid issuing pious boilerplate statements or videos that don't respond to the specific issue.
> Don't position yourself as a victim. It won't work.

I want to call your attention to this last recommendation: If you seek power, influence, and public office, you are not a victim, and you can't act like one. That's why Warren's stratagem didn't work. You don't choose the US Senate for your first run at an elected office if you want to be viewed as demure. If you insist and say you are, no one will believe you anyway.

While this holds true for men seeking political power, it is especially true for you, the woman who does. That's because you're already acting against type. Your desire for power tips off your constituents from the get-go. So have faith that the voters and decision makers will think past your transgressions (actual or perceived) and remember why they want you to have power.

Voters, regardless of political persuasion, basically want the world to be a better place. Use language that is aspirational and inspirational. You need to express (you should forgive the expression) the audacity of hope, not your insecurities or fears. Even when, or especially when, the news is totally dismal, your job is to tell people that you will partner with them to make sure that this terrible thing will never happen again and that you have solutions to their problems.

Strategic imperatives for rolling with the punches:

★ Make sure your political consultant is a communications expert, or has the cell number of a crisis communications expert at hand.

★ When a reporter says you're outspoken, just say, "I can't help it. I care so much."

★ Deliver your bad news on Friday afternoon, when reporters and constituents are thinking about their weekend and not about you.

★ Keep your fears to yourself. If you have to talk to someone, pick just one person for anytime you need to talk, so that your secrets are kept in the tightest of circles.

★ Surround yourself with girlfriends who care about what you care about and think about the world of public life the same way you do.

★ Rough up your thin skin. Debbie Wasserman Schultz tells *Elle* magazine, "After twenty years in office, I have the skin of an alligator."

★ Don't ever show embarrassment. You may be sorry, but you're not mortified. Always remember you're no more fallible than anyone else.

★ If you consistently do good, others will give you a pass when you do bad. If you doubt this truth, think about Bill Clinton.

★ When all else fails, haul out the pink sweater.

31

Time is not on your side; use it or lose it

Time is a resource, and thinking about time as inventory will help enforce the discipline a winning campaign needs. Every minute really does count. Thinking this way enables you to focus only on what really matters. And that is how you will win.

Some girls are lucky. No, not because they are born rich or famous—they are lucky because they seem to know just what they want to do when they grow up. One of these girls is US senator Amy Klobuchar, a Democrat from Minnesota who dreams of being ever more politically powerful—maybe even president one day.

Of course, Klobuchar has never publicly said, "I want to be president." But no one ever does. Indeed, some outright deny it to throw the rest of us off the scent. Then they run for president anyway. In October 2006, *Washington Post* reporter Dan Balz wrote, "Until yesterday, Obama, one of the brightest stars in the party since he electrified the 2004 Democratic National Convention with his keynote address, had said he planned to serve out the full six years of his Senate term, which would have ruled out a presidential or vice presidential campaign in 2008."

Others, like Amy Klobuchar, attempt to disarm but don't deny.

In a 2010 profile for *Elle*, several women asked Klobuchar when she would run for president. "Yeah, yeah, right," Klobuchar said. When pressed, she continued, "Right now, I'm going to announce that I'm getting some food." No denial there.

By the time she was in her forties, in her first term in the Senate, Klobuchar was appearing on lists of women who might be the first woman president. And they weren't just any old lists. But Klobuchar didn't get on the *New York Times*'s list because she was lucky. She got on it because once she realized she wanted a life in politics, she started working her tail off to get it.

Klobuchar's approach involves a "confront, co-opt, control" strategy, but it's different from those we've seen so far here. Her strategy is subtler: meet everybody (confront), make friends with everybody (co-opt), and then recruit everyone to your campaign (control). Her strategy feels so friendly that no one realizes she's using her time to the fullest and just as ambitiously as propriety will permit. Then she softens everyone up with humor.

For instance, during her own 2012 reelection campaign, Klobuchar traveled to Iowa to campaign. During the Democratic National Convention, she attended an Iowa delegation breakfast, a do-not-miss event for would-be presidential candidates. "I can see Iowa from my porch," she said, disarmingly. Klobuchar continued: "You have Albert, the world's largest bull; we have the world's largest ball of twine. . . . You are the state that makes or breaks presidents; and, to invoke the names of Hubert Humphrey and Walter Mondale, we are the state that makes vice presidents that run for president."

Here is how she does it: Klobuchar understood early on that she needed to build a constituency of friends who could become her voters, fast. (Being a senator—not to mention the president—requires a whole lot of voters.)

Valedictorian of her high school class in Wayzata, Minnesota, Klobuchar graduated from Yale magna cum laude in political science in 1982. Her senior essay was published as a textbook, *Uncovering the Dome*, and is still used in college classrooms all over the country. The topic? Politics, of course. At the University of Chicago Law School, Klobuchar was an associate editor of the *Law Review*, which is where I ran into her. My husband was the articles editor and noted Klobuchar's wit and also her ambition. There was no doubt in his mind that Klobuchar had a plan and that she was executing it.

After law school, Klobuchar moved home to Minnesota to recruit the next group of voters. She began climbing the political ladder, running for office and recruiting for her campaigns for Hennepin county attorney. Among Klobuchar's earliest recruits were law school classmates she asked to fund her campaigns, and my husband and I were among those who donated. (I've given to the campaigns of many of the women I write about in this book.) Though at first my husband and I wondered whether this was money we needed to spend, we soon had no worries. Once again, Klobuchar was executing, but good. Occasionally we would read the reports she sent to donors. We would also hear from friends in Minneapolis and Saint Paul about her good work.

Klobuchar climbed that political ladder with the discipline that winning campaigns need—planning out every day, acting on the understanding that every minute counts, thinking only about what really matters. For instance, early in her first campaign for the US Senate, Klobuchar asked my husband and me to introduce her to fellow Chicagoans. If it had been anyone else, I would have said, "Let's wait a while. No one here has ever heard of you. It's just kind of early in the process." But we understood Klobuchar's ambition and that our friendship was something she could call on. Why not now? A handful of people showed up, of course, but years later attendees thank me for making that introduction. A winning campaign is about focusing on how to confront, co-opt, and control the voters as early as you can, so they don't even consider voting for anyone but you.

One of Klobuchar's favorite stories is about her early political days as a student intern for vice president Walter Mondale. But this story doesn't involve important research Klobuchar did for the vice president, nor is it about her diligence in taking notes for him at meetings, though I'm sure she did both.

No, this story is about crawling under the vice president's desk.

Apparently, Klobuchar was assigned the task of inventorying the vice president's office furniture, and she had to crawl under the desk to record inventory numbers.

Is this cute story designed to lighten up a stump speech? Hardly. Cute isn't what a senator wants to communicate about herself. "That was my first job in Washington," she says in a 2010 article in *Elle* titled "The Audacity of Minnesota."

By telling it, Klobuchar demonstrates her arrival at the seat of power at a young age. It indicates her willingness to do whatever needs doing. (I like that in my candidates; I can identify with it.) And it illustrates her understanding of what's important—serving those who need your help. (I sure like that in my senators and my presidents, too.)

By realizing she needed to make every minute count, and then actually making every minute count, Klobuchar gets to tell a story that reinforces the righteousness of her ultimate Election Day. Pure genius. Nothing cute about it. If it's already too late for you to start as early as Klobuchar did, don't worry about it. There's no point in worrying about things you can't control.

You can, however, understand and take to heart what Klobuchar did: make a plan for each day, and execute that plan with discipline. Once you've decided on your Election Day, time's a-wasting if you don't.

Most people spend their lives living for the weekend—living through five days to get to the two days they feel are theirs. Not you. Like Klobuchar, every day is your day because every day is a campaign day, filled with stories about you.

Organizing your time—and your life—in this way is a lot of work. You will need to be on your toes every minute of every day, and you will need to say no to some of the fun stuff your friends propose.

Let's go back to Klobuchar's story about inventorying the vice presidential furniture and the messages it evokes for us, her voters. As I mentioned, one important message is Klobuchar's willingness to do whatever needs doing. You, too, always want to convey that message. But just like television, a campaign has prime time, and the definition of prime time is exactly the same, too: it's when the most people are watching. This means that as you plan your campaign stops, you want to stop at the right time. So, while you're willing to do whatever needs doing, you will be making some choices about when. Here's how to think about this.

First, the measure of what's a prime-time activity is not always the same. For instance, crawling under desks to inventory furniture would hardly seem like a prime-time activity, but when you're working in the vice president's office or any other important place, even the most insignificant-seeming activities take on greater meaning. In those sorts of places, your only prime-time task is to do whatever is requested because the request is made by someone who may be uniquely important to you later on. Make sure you know when you're in one of these places when you're doing your campaign planning.

Second, some activities can only be done in prime time. Say you're asked to speak to the PTA at an evening meeting, but you've also got lots of Girl Scout troop-donor thank-you letters to personalize and sign. Remember this: you can sign those thank-you letters at midnight, but you can't meet your sister PTA members, your new voters, then.

Third, some activities are best done in prime time. Make sure you know which ones, and schedule them accordingly. Say you're invited to meet someone important. Best to meet that person during prime time: you'll have the chance to maximize the value of that contact by meeting others at her office and co-opting them, too. Oh, you say it would be better to meet at Starbucks after five, after you've picked up your kids from school? Not a good call. Ask a friend to pick up the kids. Oh, you say you have a class you don't want to miss? Ask someone to take notes for you.

Last, some campaign projects don't ever need to be done in prime time. Not only can you sign those donor letters at midnight, you can stuff envelopes for the garden club and swim team at midnight. You can draft that PTA speech at midnight. You can read those class notes at midnight. You can send a thoughtful e-mail at midnight. You can research and plan your next day at midnight (the Internet was made for this). Last but certainly not least, you can commiserate with your girlfriends and call your campaign advisers at midnight. What good are they if they're not there for you 24/7? Don't ever waste your prime time. Use it to your fullest advantage, both for your present and for your future, just as Klobuchar did when she crawled under that vice presidential desk that day.

Strategic imperatives for achieving great ratings in prime time:

★ Seek media placement in media that is syndicated, so that your name is mentioned in many contexts simultaneously.

★ A note written by hand, even if it is short, has a much greater impact than an e-mail. Any time you spend hand-writing is well worth it.

★ Don't spend time obsessing about not having the latest electronic gadget, when all you need to be able to do is send e-mails. The point is to touch people, not the technology you use to do it.

★ Figure out when you have the most—and the least—energy during the day, and plan your day to maximize it.

A big Election Day is
never the end of the road

If you view every day as part of your ongoing campaign, you will have innumerable chances to create momentum for the next Election Day. Even after serving at the pinnacle of national American politics, former secretaries of state Madeleine Albright and Condoleezza Rice continue to travel the world, inspiring women and girls everywhere.

Every day is Election Day and each victory is a stepping stone to the next one. Molly Bordonaro was only twenty-seven when she first ran (unsuccessfully) for Congress in Oregon in 1996. She ran again in 1998, and though she lost that race too, she still made a splash. And she made the most of it politically; it led to her becoming an ambassador. "Losing the race was jarring, but you don't lose the desire to make your community better."

Two years later, George W. Bush invited Bordonaro to work on his first presidential campaign. In 2000 she went on to serve as chair of the Pacific states for the Bush-Cheney presidential campaign and in 2004 as the Northwest regional chair. During those years, she also served as a member of the US Congressional Commission on the Advancement of Women in Science and Technology.

In 2005, Bordonaro became Bush's ambassador to Malta. Like many ambassador appointees, she had been a significant campaign fundraiser. Unlike most, she was quite young. At thirty-six, she was the youngest woman ambassador ever. Bordonaro's youngest child was five months old when the family arrived in Malta, where her husband became a self-described stay-at-home dad. Bordonaro says, "I embraced that opportunity to talk to young women about having career dreams. Don't be held back by perceived cultural obstacles."

A political appointment, that job came to an end with the election of Barack Obama in 2008. Bordonaro returned home to Portland, where she resumed her career in commercial real estate development.

From political up-and-comer to political insider to powerful businesswoman—each of Bordonaro's steps could have been a career in itself, but each step along the path contributed to her suitability for the next one. As Bordonaro says, "I don't believe you get one shot, have one chapter. There's always an opportunity to have impact."

Ludmyrna "Myrna" Lopez, a child of Mexican immigrants, was born in Berkeley, California, and grew up in the nearby town of Richmond, where she attended an all-girl Catholic high school. To satisfy the school's community-service requirement, Lopez played music at homes for the elderly and worked at a food bank. But she also demonstrated an early interest in politics. In college, she worked as an intern in the office of a local state assembly member. She now says that that experience opened her eyes and led directly to her later choices. "I did constituent work. I had to be responsive to the community. It opened my eyes [to the good government could do]."

Lopez went to college at California State in Hayward, where she won a graduate school fellowship for students of color studying public policy. Then, after a summer program in public policy, she went to Pittsburgh for graduate school. Though it was the first time Lopez had ever left home, she says she chose Carnegie Mellon because she had discovered that many of its graduates ended up in Washington. She wanted that, too, so she figured out how to make it happen.

"I was there for six years impacting public policy at the national level," working at the Environmental Protection Agency on economic development plans. When she returned home to Richmond, Lopez's commitment to public policy didn't waver. She served as the city's planning commissioner for four years and was subsequently elected a member of the city council.

Public policy, says Lopez, is the process of making and implementing proposals for government to be more effective. By contrast, Lopez says, public service takes a variety of forms: elected official, appointed official, community activist, and leader of civic organizations, such as the one she headed, the Contra Costa program of Women's Initiative for Self Employment.

"My work at Women's Initiative was part and parcel of my world: to empower low-income people." Keeping her eye on that political prize, Lopez added, "If you're more economically secure, you can be civically engaged. Women's Initiative enabled me to stay out there and help the clients succeed."

In 2010, when Lopez ran for reelection to the Richmond, California, city council, she lost. She says the Richmond City Council "was perfect for me. I knew government and policy and public service." During her first term, Lopez was, she says herself, the "fresh-faced, home-grown girl." Nevertheless, she was defeated in her second campaign.

When I asked Lopez about the prospect of running for office, she demurred but emphasized that "I can help make people's lives better" in whatever she does. Today, she does that in part by working in the Alameda County Administrator's Office on its Women's Hall of Fame project.

When I asked Molly Bordonaro whether she'd run for office again, she said, "I'm very open to thinking big, even if it's ten years down the road."

Myrna Lopez's parents emigrated from Guanajuato in Mexico. They had little education and couldn't speak English. They started their American lives in the most modest of circumstances. Molly Bordonaro's parents were educated and financially successful. But both families taught their girls to be resourceful. This has come in handy as each has pursued several public careers.

Bordonaro says, "Life is a journey of lots of bumps. There is always an opportunity to have an impact, so don't ever feel that time slips away."

In other words, it's never too late to try again.

Strategic imperatives for continuous Election Days:

★ Make sure your dream is not an emotional all or nothing.

★ Identify the steps along the path that suffice and take great pleasure in making them.

★ Find joy in the smaller experiences along your way, especially in your interaction with others, versus your self-satisfaction (even if you're self-satisfied because you achieved something significant). Joy in and for others is truly a gift.

★ If these joyful experiences can be repeated, repeat them.

There's no success like failure

The political girl knows that winning is the best outcome, but losing isn't the worst. Even if you lose, you can position yourself for the next round. The right attitude is not "I helped to make the process better" or "I helped to raise some issues; now I'm going back to walk my dog and cook dinner for my family." It's "I'm here, and I'm not going anywhere. I may have a different job, but I'm still fighting for what women need. And I will be back."

Winning the next Election Day will be a matter of developing a new platform and message so that you stay in the public eye and so that what you do matters. Once you've accomplished that, you can declare a victory.

This is what winners do. They launch their next campaign as soon after the current loss as possible, in order to retain the momentum and visibility their efforts have created. They know they get another shot, but it has to come hard on the last one.

This may be why Sarah Palin wanted to make her own speech the night John McCain lost the race for president in 2008. Though this is usually not done, I'm guessing this young woman who had vaulted from obscurity to international fame in three short months when McCain selected her as his runningmate, wanted to hang on to her fame and continue to be a player. "Bright lights, big city (gone to my baby's head)" is how the old blues song goes.

In the case of Hillary Clinton, immediately after she lost the Democratic primary to Barack Obama, she became a fervent and loyal supporter. She made the judgment that an Obama win was better for her and her future voters than a McCain win. Though this wasn't a hard call on the issues and though Clinton has always been a team player, it must have been a difficult move to make. Nevertheless, she made it: Clinton is a big girl and an ambitious one. And she knew that supporting Obama would put her back in national play right away. She was appointed secretary of state in short order.

A lot of Election Days, like this one, involve losing and winning at the same time. Myrna Lopez talked about her difficult loss when she ran for reelection for city council in Richmond, California. Betsy Gotbaum contemplated a run for mayor of New York City, but it wasn't in the cards. Yet, both created new platforms for themselves quickly and put themselves right back out there.

Toni Preckwinkle talks about how hard it was for the better part of her two years running for president of the Cook County Board of Commissioners, when no one thought she had a shot and a lot of big boys and big girls did not take her calls. This is a different version of the same phenomenon. Preckwinkle was losing during all those months, losing money and endorsements that could have made her path to victory easier. But by the time Election Day came, she had won them, and so she won on Election Day. Sometimes the campaign is just harder and longer than you think it ought to be, and there are more mountains to climb on the path. "Lord, don't move the mountain, but give me the strength to climb," sang gospel singer Inez Andrews.

Stories of loss abound in the political world, even among victors. As Carol Bellamy puts it, "There's no silver in politics." She is right when it comes to a particular campaign's Election Day. But then there is the next day, when you pick yourself up, dust yourself off, reassert your presence in the public eye, and start your next campaign. Sharon Broome says this about losing a legislative fight, even an important one: "I'm a big girl. I just shake it off and go on about my business."

Cheryle Robinson Jackson ran for the Illinois Democratic primary nomination for US Senate. When she lost, she used her newfound public voice to establish herself as a leader of the national movement to increase the number of women in elected office. Given the competition she faced, I'm not sure Jackson thought she really had a chance to win. I never asked her, because I was sure she understood that if she ran a credible race, she'd have traction for the future, including positioning herself for her next Election Day. Sometimes it's worth campaigning for a bigger office than your resumé seems to merit or your supporters think is prudent. Consider it. If you do, you will distinguish yourself from the crowd seeking the job. That's where you want to be, always and all ways.

Catherine ("Cathy" when she and I worked together as young women) Bertini lost a run for Congress in Illinois but parlayed her execution of a credible campaign against a long-term incumbent into appointment to a significant state public office. From there, it was on to bigger and bigger appointed positions, including at the US Department of Agriculture and then as the (first woman and first American) director of the United Nations World Food Programme (at age forty-two). Later, she was appointed by UN secretary general Kofi Annan to the position of UN undersecretary general for management, responsible for the agency's $3 billion administrative operation. Today, she is a senior stateswoman, appointed by the Democrats she once opposed. There is also a long list of honorary degrees next to her name.

Susan Molinari was a successful three-term member of Congress from New York when she resigned to become a TV anchor. Subsequently, she was a lobbyist and government relations professional, working with some of the biggest names in the business. Fifteen years (many lifetimes in politics) after her resignation from Congress, Molinari became head of Google's office in Washington, DC. That's quite a comeback for someone who was criticized for leaving public office and whose media career received mixed reviews.

My favorite example of losing but winning features US senator Barbara Mikulski and her leadership of a campaign at the center of every

American working woman's life: the one to obtain equal pay for equal work.

In 2012, Mikulski was the sponsor in the Senate of the Paycheck Fairness Act, which, according to CNN, "would require employers to prove that differences in pay were related to job performance, not gender; would prevent employers from forbidding employees from sharing salary information with each other; and would allow women who believe they were discriminated against to sue for damages."

The measure was defeated on a procedural vote when no Republican, including none of the four Republican women senators, voted for the bill. Mikulski had lost, but she wasn't having it. She said she understood that the Republican women senators were under a gag order and that "they do stand for equal pay and paycheck fairness." Then she looked ahead and said, "We will be back. Though we lost the vote today we are not giving up. The fight for equal pay will continue. This is a fight for fairness. . . . Suit up, put lipstick on, square shoulders. . . . I am comeback-ready to keep on fighting."

"Comeback-ready" is the drill when you want to be the kind of marine Mikulski is.

When I was writing this book, I learned that many women political leaders were Girl Scouts. In their formative years, all had learned the Girl Scout Promise: "On my honor, I will try to do my duty to God and my country, to help other people at all times, and to obey the Girl Scout Law."

When I was a Girl Scout, I recited it. Later, I learned my parents, including my mother, who was my Brownie troop leader, did not like the word "try." When I came home from school with a B instead of an A, I said, "I tried to get an A." They weren't having it. Go back and get (not "try to get") an A.

However, sometimes you do try as hard as you can, but there is no gold medal to be had. I think that is exactly why the Girl Scout Promise states that there is value in trying. I recommend it. Try as hard and as smart as you can every time you have an Election Day. If you lose, try again. On the evening of Election Day, announce your new plan and go at it the next morning.

When you do this, you will want to make your case for the new campaign personally, if not in person, to your most important supporters. A telephone call or an e-mail will do. Tell each person why you see this loss as having positioned you well for your next Election Day, which, you're just certain, they will want to be a part of, too. After all, no one likes to see a good investment go bad. Sometimes more venture capital is needed than was originally projected.

Deanna Archuleta returned to New Mexico after a stint in Washington, DC, because she missed the "sense of place" her home state gives her. She also knew her children were ready to return home. And she says, "I feel like I can make a bigger difference locally. Careers are made when these kinds of decisions arise." You, too, can return to the kind of Election Day best suited to you.

Strategic imperatives for making the most of a setback:

★ Analyze your loss to identify the elements that were instrumental in that loss.

★ Determine whether you can win absent those elements, and if so, make an alternate plan for your next race.

★ Turn out the next day after an Election Day loss and make your (new) case for winning.

★ If there is no winning recipe, reevaluate this element of your plan. Is there another office that would satisfy you and in which you could make a difference? Monica Banks realized she could run for chancery clerk, though being circuit clerk had been a long-held dream. Think like Monica thought.

★ If you land on a positive alternative, quickly identify the people who were instrumental to your achieving it and let them know your intentions. Then they, too, can announce your good news—you're back.

On loyalty, which
supersedes everything

Turnout and loyalty are the coin of the political realm. That's why this book begins with turnout and ends with loyalty. You can't win on Election Day without both firmly in place. And they're related, of course: when you turn out for others, and they do the same for you, you build loyalty to each other. And loyalty is what you need most when you are dreaming big.

Clearly, you're a loyal person. Why else would you keep turning up? You make it to all those community meetings because you're loyal to your community, and in return you seek the community's loyalty on your Election Day.

And if you remain loyal to your convictions, even if your opposition disagrees with them, they'll respect you for your consistency and character.

Perhaps you're starting your political career as a young mother, the way political activists Bettylu Saltzman and Deanna Archuleta did—organizing other young mothers in your neighborhood. Perhaps you attend candidate meetings and contribute time or money to candidates you believe in. Perhaps you started out as a political campaign staffer, as Laura Tucker did, or as a young professional woman with political aspirations, as Catherine Kimball and Sharon Broome did. As you do, the minute you do, you build loyalty.

Maybe, a few years down the road, your favorite candidate loses badly. Is that the time to jump ship? Of course not. You are a loyal person. You stuck with her even when she made a decision you didn't like. Likewise, she took your calls when you had a bone to pick and listened as you made your case. This is no time to destroy that intimacy.

When the time comes—and it will, I assure you—that the official or candidate you support behaves badly, hurting her own reputation and embarrassing you, is that when you take a hike, or does loyalty trump embarrassment? Yes indeed, it does.

There's a story about Louisiana governor Earl Long where he's been having a really bad day and an aide said, "I'm with you when you're right, Governor. But not when you're wrong." Long is said to have replied, "You stupid son of a bitch. I don't need you when I'm right!"

Loyalty gives you counselors and supporters you can trust, which you'll need at the low points as well as the high. From the standpoint of your family member, friend, candidate, or supporter, if you can't be depended upon, your other attributes don't matter. Smart people can be replaced by other smart people. Hard workers can be replaced by other hard workers. But loyalty, built over time, is unique. And if you abrogate loyalty when times turn tough, it will be close to impossible to build that trust back. And if you do it once, you might do it twice. There's no room for trust in a relationship like that, and trust is key if you want to be present in the small rooms where the decisions get made.

Saltzman has been in the political game for decades. She's still smiling, even though many candidates she has supported have lost, and the pace she maintains is fast. Her telephone is constantly ringing, and then she's (constantly) ringing you. People in politics want her because she epitomizes the "no coffee break" approach you need to win on Election Day. With iPhone in hand, laptop charged up and ready to go for the holidays, and donor lists catalogued, she has fun, but she never forgets her to-do list.

When I volunteer to raise money for a candidate, Saltzman is the first person I call. When I organize an advocacy campaign for a cause, Saltzman is the first person I call. That's because I know she's loyal. She doesn't stop going to meetings when the candidate hits a bad spot. She doesn't stop fund-raising when the candidate says something dumb. She doesn't stop believing when the candidate's handlers are lost. She remains loyal. That's the supporter you want, too.

I was a member of a group of donors to an official we had all supported enthusiastically. A disenchanted friend of some of the group's members proposed that we withdraw our financial support. A letter was drafted and shared at lunch one day, and I told the group I wouldn't participate.

Here's what I was thinking: on balance, this official has taken policy positions I like—a lot. She has advocated for legislation I think is valuable. There has been a lot of good in her record of public service. I also have a personal relationship with her that I value. I consider the women politicians I support family. Families make up and move on. Having the ability, partly supplied by their supporters, to pick themselves up and get back in the game is what will get candidates in a rough patch to Election Day quickest. And as their supporter, that's what I want for them.

It is easy to understand the value of constant loyalty to someone who shares your views, at least most of the time. However, what should you do if she radically changes her views on an important issue, even the issue that brought you to her side in the first place? This is a tough call, because many of us got involved—and stay involved—in politics in order to advance policies that benefit women. Consequently, when an official or a candidate flails—no, bails—my loyalty is challenged. Then I remember: Flailing and bailing go with this territory. Compromise goes with this territory. Being opportunistic goes with this territory. Even being evasive goes with this territory.

If you only want to be loyal to saints, politics is not for you. If you want to be a saint, politics is definitely not for you.

If you have decided instead that you're good with people who do the right thing most of the time, then make sure you ask them to do the same for you in return. She'll get what she wants. You'll get what you want.

This book is full of advice about weaving a safety net that will keep you from falling into the abyss, but disloyalty tears holes in the net that will be very hard to mend.

Over the years, I have learned a lot about loyalty from Saltzman. When I've expressed frustration to her about the decision some politician we support has made, she's replied that if you support someone because her values are aligned with yours, you should remain loyal. Saltzman says, "It's a civic duty to have the right people represent us."

Saltzman puts this belief into action and reaps the rewards that come from it. She rarely says no to a request to raise money and, unlike most of her peers, actually does door-to-door precinct work. She celebrated President Obama's fiftieth birthday grooving to Stevie Wonder with a couple hundred other people on the South Lawn of the White House.

Dancing with the one who brung you underpins most of the arguments I'm making here.

Even though I broke off with a women's group I founded and they with me, I later re-engaged with members because I still valued their loyalty to me and my causes, as I knew they wanted mine for theirs. We had spent a lifetime caring about the same things, though this one project had failed. For me, this experience is the exception that proves the rule. Sometimes you can go home again, but it's rare. So don't count on it.

Loyalty is even more important when you're the candidate. If you're honest and unyielding about your political ambition and your right to have a voice in the public square, you are entitled to the same respect as anyone else on the field, and you are positioned to win without apology. You are going to fight just as hard as they do. And if you've walked the precincts for your colleagues and you've called on them to get your back, chances are you are going to win. Good luck, and get busy now.

Epilogue:
Every year is the year of the woman

★ ★ ★

American women register to vote more than men do. They also vote more than men do. Women of every kind and from everywhere believe in their right to influence our world by taking this right seriously. And for decades women have taken responsibility for organizing campaigns, getting voters to the polls, running elections, and making sure that their concerns are addressed by local governments.

Back in the 1950s my mother was an active volunteer in local Democratic politics. She was our local woman representative to the New York State Democratic Party. I remember her driving people to the polls, with us kids piled in the backseat. Later, she was a member of an advisory committee to the local school board, won election to the school board, and served as its president.

As I think about my mother's willingness to dive in and start swimming—five kids in tow and her own career to run—I am filled with admiration. Of course, her eagerness to find the time and put it in is not unique. Today, there are tens of thousands of women doing what she did all over the United States. They are married with children, single with children, gay, straight, conservative, liberal, and all different colors. Every neighborhood has at least a few. Recently, I was a guest on a political radio show along with an African American woman pastor. She mentioned how she and her congregants are active in their community like my mother was, and are now considering running for office.

Women who ran and won in 2012's historic elections included Tammy Duckworth, a severely disabled war veteran and now a member of Congress; Tammy Baldwin, now the first openly gay US senator; Claire McCaskill, now a second-term US senator, who faced down a man who said there was such a thing as "legitimate rape"; Debbie Stabenow, the first Democratic woman to move from the US House of Representatives to the US Senate; Heidi Heitkamp, a pro-Keystone XL pipeline Democrat, now US senator from North Dakota; Mazie Hirono, the first Asian American woman and first Buddhist US senator; Tulsi Gabbard, the first Hindu in the US House of Representatives; and Cathy McMorris Rodgers, the highest-ranking woman in Congress and only woman in the House of Representatives Republican leadership. Among losers who ran hard, well, and close was Mia Love, who was born to Jamaican immigrants in Brooklyn, New York, and who became a Mormon, a Utah mayor, and a powerful candidate for US Congress.

And as of 2012 in New Hampshire, the governor, Maggie Hassan, and the entire federal delegation were female. In other states, eight women are state senate presidents, and six women are speakers of their states' houses.

I'm no Pollyanna, but I do become starry-eyed when I think about an American future with more and more women in public leadership. Even though our numbers in the halls of power won't reflect our proportion of the population for many decades to come, we will be increasingly present and accounted for.

Every summer I attend the Van Buren County Youth Fair in Michigan. One of the community buildings on the fairgrounds contains all the 4-H Club exhibits. The fair's main events are on Saturday, when the 4-Hers receive their awards and they and their families watch the demolition derby and then head for the carnival rides. At the start of the demolition derby, we stand on the hill overlooking the race track, turn to face the American flag waving at the top of the hill, and sing "The Star-Spangled Banner."

In the summer of 2012, before the singing and crashing cars started, I walked around the other community buildings, where local organizations and businesses set up information booths. In 2012, the Van Buren County Democratic Party was selling Michelle Obama buttons at its booth, and I bought a couple. One says Keep Michelle First Lady. No Matter How She Combs It, She Is Our First Lady was the other, which showed Obama in five hairstyles and featured a pink heart as its centerpiece.

Inside the booth, a flyer entitled: "It's Time for a Change" caught my eye. Below that headline were pictures of three Democratic women—Shelia Johnson, Connie Marie Kelley, and Bridget Mary McCormack, running for election to the Michigan Supreme Court. On the other side of the flyer was a big headline: "Debbie Stabenow: Fighting for Michigan," next to a picture of Stabenow looking all business. Four women clearly in charge and running for high office were the big excitement for me that day at the Van Buren County Fair.

The next time you attend a community event, look around for the political women. If you're one yourself, look for the others. Then get together and remind yourself, as the Michigan judges did when they decided to run together: every year is the year of the woman. Help each other remember that when women run, women win.

Resources:
Get busy now

★ ★ ★

You're inspired, you're courageous, you're ready to go. Time to muster your resources. Here are the sources and the information you'll need to get you started down the right path.

While all candidates need some things—aptitude and fortitude, for starters—you won't all have the same tools. For instance, campaigns differ due to the type of office sought, the scope of its responsibility, and the size of the electorate. Therefore, as you undertake this career and climb this career ladder, you will have to create a new strategic plan at each step on the ladder. The resources here will help you do that.

For instance, in the fund-raising section, you'll find information about many different kinds of fund-raising and how to sort out which one is right for you and for which campaign. In the section on training programs, you will find links to training programs for prospective candidates with differing levels of experience, and links to specific tactical skills, such as how to staff a campaign (you can never do it alone), even if your "staff" is friends and colleagues because the office you're seeking is a starter office.

Here is some of the subject matter covered by the organizations listed below:

★ Becoming a leader and training to win

★ Organizing your campaigns

★ Developing and promoting your brand and message

★ Becoming a member of everything that will help ensure your success

197

★ Raising money from everyone

★ Learning the issues that will matter

★ Keeping up with the competition (which is mostly other women)

★ Knowing what the pundits know, sharing your views with them, and becoming a pundit yourself

★ Becoming a citizen of the world

At the end of this section, you will find lists of books and movies about politics.

Time to dig in.

Becoming a Leader and Training to Win

★ ★ ★

Political Skills Training for Running for Elected and Appointed Office

Seeking and winning office is not a DIY project. All kinds of people will be able to help you, and you'll know just what to ask them for, as well as what to reasonably ask of yourself, once you complete training before launching your campaign.

Center for American Women and Politics (CAWP)
Eagleton Institute of Politics
Rutgers, The State University of New Jersey
191 Ryders Lane
New Brunswick, NJ 08901-8557
(732) 932-9384; fax (732) 932-6778
www.cawp.rutgers.edu

"Ready to Run™ is a non-partisan campaign training program to encourage women to run for elective office, position themselves for appointive office, work on a campaign, or get involved in public life in other ways. Central to the Ready to Run™ model is an innovative, comprehensive curriculum that incorporates the political culture and climate of the locale and uses state and local campaign experts to highlight the specifics of running in a particular state or region. The program demystifies the process of running for elected office, encourages more women to mount campaigns, and introduces them to elected and appointed leaders, campaign consultants, and party officials in their state to whom they can turn as they get ready to run. CAWP's model curriculum covers fund-raising, positioning oneself for elected office, navigating the political party structure, media training, the nuts and bolts of organizing a campaign, mobilizing voters, and crafting a message."

The program has two tracks: "I'm Ready to Run, Now What" and "I'm Not Ready to Run Yet, But . . ." There are also special programs for women of color: "Eleccion Latina, Rising Stars," "Educating Asian American Women for Politics," and "Run Sister Run: Women of the African Diaspora Changing the Political Landscape." And there's a program for college women interested in politics called "The New Leaderships."

The CAWP website offers an interactive map of the United States listing training programs and related resources state by state: *CAWP Political and Leadership Resources for Women*, www.cawp.rutgers.edu/education_training /trainingresources/index.php, including state programs of Emerge, www .emergeamerica.org.

The CAWP website also lists and describes programs that train college women, women only, men and women, only Democrats, and only Republicans. Here is the link to information about campaign training for women: www.cawp.rutgers.edu/education_training/ReadytoRun/National _Training_Network.php.

The presentations that were offered at CAWP's 2012 Southern Regional Women's Public Leadership Summit will give you a good sense of what to expect from CAWP. These PowerPoint presentations can be downloaded at cawp.rutgers.edu/site/pages/SouthernSummit-slides.php.

★ Kelly Dittmar, Center for American Women and Politics (CAWP), "From the Last Year of the Woman to 2012"

★ Cate Gormley, Lake Research Partners (for the Voter Participation Center), "The Power of Women"

★ Barbara Rackes, Southeastern Institute for Women in Politics, "Game Plan for Mobilizing Women in South Carolina"

★ Alysia Snell, Lake Research Partners (for the Barbara Lee Family Foundation), "Messages That Work for Women Candidates"

Your criteria for selecting a training program should include consideration of the following issues: level of office you are seeking, whether you prefer party-specific training or not; the skills you need to learn most; and how much training you have the time, money, and/or interest for.

Night School
Democracy for America
PO Box 1717
Burlington, VT 05402
(802) 651-3200; fax (802) 651-3299
www.democracyforamerica.com

"DFA Night School is our online training program that allows anyone to learn the skills to win from their own home. Each session is an interactive video web conference where trainees participate and ask questions. Featuring expert trainers, topics range from 'Volunteer Recruitment' to 'Framing a Message' to 'Fund-raising' to 'Online Media.'"

New Organizing Institute
1133 19th Street NW, Suite 850
Washington, DC 20036
(202) 558-5585; fax (202) 204-6290
www.neworganizing.com
E-mail: info@neworganizing.com

The Candidate Training Project is a program of the New Organizing Institute that trains activists to seek local office. Training resources are online, and training sessions are held in conjunction with Democracy for America (see above). Sessions and materials cover all aspects of running, beginning with answering the question, "Should I run for office?"

Running Start
1111 16th Street NW, Suite 420
Washington, DC 20035
(202) 223-3895; fax (202) 223-4136
www.runningstartonline.org
www.runningstartonline.org/programs/young-womens-political-leadership
E-mail: info@runningstartonline.org

"We are dedicated to inspiring young women to run for political office. Running Start's programs give young women the knowledge, support, encouragement, and inspiration they need to run for an elected position."

Women's Campaign Fund
1900 L Street NW, Suite 500
Washington, DC 20036
(202) 393-8164; fax (202) 393-0649
www.wcfonline.org

The Women's Campaign Fund (WCF), "a nonpartisan organization," is dedicated to "dramatically increasing the number of women in elected office who support reproductive health choices for all." WCF's operations include She Should Run, www.sheshouldrun.org, and a political action committee (PAC). (See below for more on PACs.)

Local Political Skills Training Opportunities

Local sources for political skills training include the political parties; the League of Women Voters; chapters and affiliated projects of national organizations like the AAUW, the NAACP, the National Council of LaRaza, and the Asian American Legal Defense and Education Fund (www.aaldef.org; website addresses for other previously mentioned groups are found elsewhere in this section); women's professional societies and trade associations; and leadership training programs at local community colleges or other adult education programs.

Community Organizing and Political Campaign Training

Many women seeking public leadership positions and running for office begin their careers as community activists working on all kinds of issues and causes. The skills you will learn are translatable directly to the political world, whether you begin as a staffer, a volunteer, or a candidate.

Here are some organizations I recommend:

Midwest Academy
27 E. Monroe, 11th Floor
Chicago, IL 60603
(312) 427-2304; fax (312) 379-0313
www.midwestacademy.com

New Organizing Institute
1850 M Street NW, Suite 1100
Washington, DC 20036
(202) 558-5585; fax (202) 204-6290
www.neworganizing.com
E-mail: info@neworganizing.com

The New Organizing Institute training covers the following topics: "organizing and leadership, online organizing, data management, campaign management, voter registration, voter contact, GOTV [get out the vote], and media."

The NOI Toolbox has "resource centers" with comprehensive curricula on all of these topics: http://neworganizing.com/toolbox/. NOI offers in-person and online courses, including this important one: "Story Telling to Move Others to Action" (toolbox@neworganizing.com).

Wellstone Action
2446 University Avenue West, Suite 170
Saint Paul, MN 55114
(651) 645-3939; fax (651) 645-5858
www.wellstone.org

"Camp Wellstone (CW) is open to anyone interested in gaining practical skills in progressive political action."

Leadership for Educational Equity
www.educationalequity.org/work/trainings

This Teach for America affiliate offers training for members to "address the diverse civic engagement interests of our LEE members. LEE's One-Day Trainings support members from a variety of backgrounds, from those interested in learning more about public leadership, campaign support, and volunteer organizing and advocacy roles to those interested in running for office, leading advocacy or organizing efforts, or pursuing high-level policy or government positions."

Leadership Training for Women

Across the country, thousands of courses are offered on women and leadership by businesses, universities, colleges, and organizations and at special programs and conferences for women. Course content differs widely, but such classes can be a useful complement to political skills training, because the focus is on building a presence, something no successful politician can lack.

If you are interesting in leadership training, look for a suitable course at your local community college, women's center, YWCA, AAUW, League of Women Voters, businesswomen's organization, Toastmasters, chamber of commerce, or other business organization. Your professional organization may offer one, too.

As leadership training has become more popular, programs have been developed for various groups, including students, Native Americans, new immigrants, women, and those interested in either conservative or progressive politics.

Here are programs for women students:

American Association of University Women/Elect Her
1111 16th Street NW
Washington, DC 20036
(202) 785-7700; fax (202) 872-1425
www.aauw.org
E-mail: connect@aauw.org

"Elect Her—Campus Women Win, a collaboration between AAUW and Running Start, encourages and trains college women to run for student government on their campuses. Elect Her acknowledges the necessity to build the pipeline of women running for office in order to diminish the long-standing political leadership gender gap."

Clare Boothe Luce Policy Institute
112 Elden Street, Suite P
Herndon, VA 20170
(703) 318-0730; fax (703) 318-8867
www.cblpi.org

"Our goal is to engage, inform, and connect conservatives across the country, with a special focus on young women who will lead and shape the future of our nation."

Feminist Majority Foundation
1600 Wilson Boulevard, Suite 801
Arlington, VA 22209
(703) 522-2214; fax (703) 522-2219
www.feministcampus.org

The Choices Campus Leadership Program of the Feminist Majority Foundation is another resource for students interested in political activism.

National Conference for College Women Student Leaders
University of Maryland
College Park, MD 20742
(800) 326-2289
www.nccwsl.org
E-mail: nccwsl@aauw.org

The National Conference for College Women Student Leaders is sponsored by AAUW (above).

Leadership Training for Diverse Groups

The Center for Progressive Leadership
1133 19th Street NW, 9th Floor
Washington, DC 20036
(202) 775-2003; fax (202) 318-0485
www.progressiveleaders.org

The Center for Progressive Leadership offers a wide variety of leadership training programs for people interested in politics.

The New American Leaders Project
666 West End Avenue, Suite 1B
New York, NY 10025
(212) 497-3481; fax (212) 472-0508
newamericanleaders.org

The New American Leaders Project focuses on immigrants who seek political leadership.

Organizing Your Campaigns

★ ★ ★

After you've taken a training course, you will have a clear sense of what's next for you if you've decided to seek public office. You'll have learned how to organize the campaign appropriate to the office you are seeking. The trainers will also direct you to experts, including your local party, who can guide you in setting up your campaign, or direct you to consultants you can retain if you're running a campaign that requires a professional staff.

If you're seeking a small, part-time office, the best advice will come from those who hold or have held the office or helped others who have sought it. You will need their support in any event.

There are also myriad websites sponsored by professional political consultants that you can study. Many of these consultants publish e-newsletters.

Here are other resources for educating yourself:

The Women's Campaign Fund publishes tip sheets for its endorsed candidates, on a variety of topics related to running a successful campaign. You can find them here: www.wcfonline.org/pages/candidates/trainings.html.

Campaigns and Elections magazine, www.campaignsandelections.com, offers a comprehensive list of campaign consultants on every imaginable facet of an electoral campaign. The list at www.campaignsandelections.com /resources/political-pages will give you a good sense of who's available.

The *National Journal*, www.nationaljournal.com, is useful for those interested in the federal government and national politics.

At this link is a great list of organizations concerned with women in politics: www.runningstartonline.org/links.

Midwest Academy published a bibliography covering topics pertinent to running for office, such as media relations, fund-raising, running a meeting, and conducting policy research, which may be found here: www.midwest academy.com/sites/default/files/Resources%20for%20Organizing.pdf

New Organizing Institute publishes the Organizer's Toolbox, which includes great guidance on a variety of topics: www.neworganizing.com/project /toolbox. A comprehensive publication, covering many aspects of running for office, may be found here: www.neworganizing.com/content/page /campaign-managers-manual.

Nonprofit Tech 2.0: A Social Media Guide for Nonprofits published "50 Nonprofits Every US Politician Should Follow on Twitter" (at non profitorgs.wordpress.com/2012/09/09/50-nonprofits-every-u-s-politican -should-follow-on-twitter), which says "Following a nonprofit on Twitter doesn't signal an endorsement. It can simply demonstrate a tiny step towards better understanding the other side's point of view."

Several how-to books are listed at the end of this section. Of course, when you attend a training session, you will receive various handbooks and workbooks.

Developing and Promoting Your Brand and Message

★ ★ ★

Participating in social media yourself and developing a brand in cyberspace are important if you are seeking a public role. Your participation will also help you develop an online network that will be instrumental to your suc-

cess. Here is a link to information about how to get started: neworganizing
.com/content/page/new-media-resources.

Your ability to be knowledgeable and a respected voice will be developed by following the writing and public and media appearances of political
writers, public intellectuals, and media personalities. There are lists of such
people below. Don't forget to pay attention to mainstream cultural events
such as new movies, TV shows, Twitter accounts, and Facebook and Google
pages, and the political actions of celebrities.

Becoming a Member of Everything That
Will Help Ensure Your Success

★ ★ ★

In part 3, "You Can Never Care Too Much," you learned about the advantage
you will gain if you join organizations and take on responsibilities and leadership roles in them. Based on where you live and the kind of public leadership role you are seeking, you will have many opportunities to choose what's
right for you. In your community, you may find local chapters of national
organizations that can provide you the opportunity to lead at the regional or
national levels as well as at the local level. Other organizations will only be
local. The key is to pick those that best serve your purposes.

You will also want to keep up with those you don't join, including knowing who their leaders are and how their work relates to yours. You will want
to engage those leaders in your work because, as you know, it's vital to public
leadership success to build supporters in as many different subsets of your
community as possible. Community events and publications and leaders will
lead you to local organizations doing valuable political and community work.

The National Council of Women's Organizations is a member coalition
representing more than 11 million American women. All of its members
are committed to advancing the status of women and girls. Many of the
organizations listed have local chapters. At www.womensorganizations.org
/index.php?option=com_content&view=article&id=20&Itemid=32, you will
be able to examine the member list by topic area.

National Council of Women's Organizations
714 G Street SE, Suite 200
Washington, DC 20003
(202) 293-4505; fax (202) 293-4507
www.womensorganizations.org

Organizations That Advocate for Women and Girls and Operate Programs Benefiting Them

In every community, there are organizations that focus on issues and services that women care about. They include the PTA, business associations, women's centers and women's studies programs at local colleges and universities, faith-based groups and institutions, sororities, girls' groups, women's professional associations, social service agencies, women's boards of community institutions like hospitals and schools, health clinics like Planned Parenthood, and civic organizations. These local groups may be chapters of national organizations. Membership in one will lead you to others. Getting involved in these organizations will also enable you to meet like-minded women who share your dreams and aspirations, work on beneficial community projects, interact with local government, and become a community leader. All of this experience will teach you about political life and what it requires. Here is a list of some of these organizations:

Association of Junior Leagues International
80 Maiden Lane, Suite 305
New York, NY 10038-4609
(212) 951-8300; fax (212) 481-7196
www.ajli.org
E-mail: info@ajli.org

Catholic Campaign for Human Development
United States Conference of Catholic Bishops
3211 Fourth Street NE
Washington, DC 20017
(202) 541-3210; fax (202) 541-3329
www.usccb.org/about/catholic-campaign-for-human-development
E-mail: cchdgrants@usccb.org

Change.org
www.change.org

Garden Club of America
14 East 60th Street, 3rd Floor
New York, NY 10022
(212) 753-8287; fax (212) 753-0134
www.gcamerica.org
E-mail: gca@gcamerica.org

Girls, Inc.
120 Wall Street
New York, NY 10005-3902
 (212) 509-2000; fax (212) 509-8708
www.girlsinc.org
E-mail: communications@girlsinc.org

Girl Scouts of the USA
420 Fifth Avenue
New York, NY 10018-2798
(800) 478-7248
www.girlscouts.org

League of Women Voters
1730 M Street NW, Suite 1000
Washington, DC 20036-4508
(202) 429-1965; fax (202) 429-0854
www.lwv.org

Moms Rising
www.momsrising.org

MoveOn.org
www.moveon.org

NAACP (National Association for the Advancement of Colored People)
4805 Mt. Hope Drive
Baltimore, MD 21215
(410) 580-5777
www.naacp.org

National Coalition on Black Civic Participation
1050 Connecticut Avenue NW, 10th Floor, Suite 1000
Washington, DC 20036
(202) 659-4929; fax (202) 659-5025
www.ncbcp.org
E-mail: ncbcp@ncbcp.org

National Council of Jewish Women
Washington Office
1707 L Street NW, Suite 950
Washington, DC 20036-4206
(202) 296-2588; fax (202) 331-7792
www.ncjw.org
E-mail: action@ncjw.org

National Council of La Raza
1126 16th Street NW, Suite 600
Washington, DC 20036-4845
(202) 785-1670; fax (202) 776-1792
www.nclr.org

National Urban League
120 Wall Street
New York, NY 10005
(212) 558-5300; fax (212) 344-5332
www.nul.org

United Methodist Women
475 Riverside Drive, 15th Floor
New York, NY 10115
(212) 870-3600
www.gbgm-umc.org/umw

Women's Funding Network
505 Sansome Street, 2nd Floor
San Francisco, CA 94111
(415) 441-0706; fax (415) 441-0827
www.womensfundingnetwork.org
E-mail: info@ womensfundingnetwork.org

YMCA of the USA
101 North Wacker Drive
Chicago, IL 60606
(800) 872-9622
www.ymca.net
E-mail: fulfillment@ymca.net

YWCA USA
2025 M Street NW, Suite 550
Washington, DC 20036
(202) 467-0801; fax (202) 467-0802
www.ywca.org
E-mail: info@ywca.org

Women's Professional Societies and Trade Associations

Women's professional organizations and trade associations are great
resources for learning about issues, becoming a leader, and building a network. Join as many as are applicable to your training and interests.

The University of Maryland maintains a Directory of Women's Professional Organizations at mith.umd.edu/WomensStudies/ReferenceRoom
/Directories/professional-organizations.html.

National Organizations That Advocate
for Women's Political Leadership

Here is a list of organizations that advocate for women's political leadership.
They vary in how much local, versus national, activity they conduct. Signing
up for their e-mail lists will enable you to determine whether joining will be
helpful to you.

Clare Boothe Luce Policy Institute
112 Elden Street, Suite P
Herndon, VA 20170
(703) 318-0730; fax (703) 318-8867
www.cblpi.org
E-mail: info@cblpi.org

The Feminist Majority Foundation
1600 Wilson Boulevard, Suite 801
Arlington, VA 22209
(703) 522-2214; fax (703) 522-2219
www.feministcampus.org

League of Women Voters
1730 M Street NW, Suite 1000
Washington, DC 20036-4508
(202) 429-1965; fax (202) 429-0854
www.lwv.org

National Organization for Women (NOW)
1100 H Street NW, Suite 300
Washington, DC 20005
(202) 628-8669
www.now.org
NOW sponsors the Young Feminist Leadership Institute, which "is a set of workshops, roundtables, and activities designed to help younger feminist leaders develop the grassroots and political organizing skills necessary to effect change in their communities."

National Women's Political Caucus
PO Box 50476
Washington, DC 20091
(202) 785-1100; fax (202) 370-6306
www.nwpc.org

Rachel's Network
1200 18th Street NW, Suite 310
Washington, DC 20036
(202) 659-0846; fax (202) 659-1333
www.rachelsnetwork.org
E-mail: info@rachelsnetwork.org

Women's National Democratic Club
1526 New Hampshire Avenue NW
Washington, DC 20036
(202) 232-7363; fax (202) 986-2791
www.democraticwoman.org

Women's National Republican Club
3 West 51st Street
New York, NY 10019
(212) 582-5454
www.wnrc.org

Membership Organizations for Women Public Officials

Once you are a public official, you will have numerous opportunities to join organizations that are focused on your field (for example, education or public utilities or health care), which help you network with your peers, enable you to build your base of supporters and your substantive expertise, and can help you become a leader in your field.

Your state, county, or municipality may have organizations of women public officials. This can be the first place to go, if you're interested in meeting other women office holders and learning firsthand what political leadership is about.

National associations of women officials also provide opportunities for members to become leaders in their states and regions, as well as nationally. The following is a list of these membership organizations, which provide educational programs and networking opportunities.

National Association of Latino Elected and Appointed Officials
1122 W. Washington Boulevard, 3rd Floor
Los Angeles, CA 90015
(213) 747-7606; fax (213) 747-7664
www.naleo.org

National Conference of State Legislatures—Women's Legislative Network
444 North Capitol Street NW, Suite 515
Washington, DC 20001
(202) 624-5400; fax (202) 737-1069
www.ncsl.org

The National Foundation for Women Legislators
910 16th Street NW, Suite 100
Washington, DC 20006
(202) 293-3040; fax (202) 293-5430
www.womenlegislators.org

The National Organization of Black Elected
Legislative Women (NOBEL-Women)
PO Box 7217
Denver, CO 80207-1217
(303) 355-7288
www.nobel-women.org
E-mail: info@nobel-women.org

Hispanic Women in Leadership
PO Box 701065
Houston, TX 77270
(713) 574-8483
www.hwil.org
E-mail: info@hwil.org

Organizations That Study Women Political Leaders

You will come to be known as an expert by taking action on the issues you care about, taking leadership roles in your community and in organizations and campaigns, and advocating and fund-raising for causes. When you decide to seek political leadership for yourself, you will appear more authoritative if you understand the history and current status of American women in politics.

Many of the organizations that study women political leaders also collect data, publish reports and articles, host educational conferences and workshops, and offer special courses on women in politics and public life. Their leaders are frequently quoted in the media on politics and women's experiences in politics. Knowing what they think and what they've learned will help you formulate your plans. Following is a selected list of these organizations.

Center for American Women and Politics (CAWP)
Eagleton Institute of Politics
Rutgers, The State University of New Jersey
191 Ryders Lane
New Brunswick, NJ 08901-8557
(732) 932-9384; fax (732) 932-6778
www.cawp.rutgers.edu

The Center for American Women and Politics publishes many useful fact sheets that you can download. These fact sheets include data on the numbers of women elected in each state, what kinds of offices women hold, the numbers of minority women who hold office, and other useful facts.

Political Parity
625 Mount Auburn Street
Cambridge, MA 02138
(617) 995-1900; fax (617) 995-1982
www.politicalparity.org

Political Parity is a nonpartisan organization seeking to "double the number of women at the highest levels of US government by 2022." It conducts research on topics such as why some states "have achieved a critical mass of elected women" and others haven't. The Barbara Lee Family Foundation supports this research, such as the project PitchPerfect: Winning Strategies for Women Candidates. The foundation may be reached at:

Barbara Lee Family Foundation
131 Mt. Auburn Street
Cambridge, MA 02138
(617) 234-0355; fax (617) 234-0357
www.barbaraleefoundation.org
E-mail: info@blff.org

She Should Run
1900 L Street NW, Suite 500
Washington, DC 20036
(202) 393-8164; fax (202) 393-0649
www.sheshouldrun.org

She Should Run has published research on women's political giving and financial resources. She Should Run also sponsors the project Name It. Change It., a bipartisan effort to call out sexist media coverage at www.nameitchangeit .org.

Women & Politics Institute
School of Public Affairs
American University
4400 Massachusetts Avenue NW
Washington, DC 20016
(202) 885-2903; fax (202) 885-2967
www.american.edu/spa/wpi
E-mail: wpi@american.edu

The Women & Politics Institute is home to Jennifer Lawless, who has written extensively about why women run for office. I highly recommend her work. In the list of books below, you'll see an entry for Lawless's latest work.

Raising Money

★ ★ ★

It may seem counterintuitive, but the most generous Americans by percentage of income, are not the richest. This means that when you're starting out, however small an office you seek, and however modest your campaign budget, you will be able to raise money. For here's the other truth: there are givers and there are nongivers. This personal trait is unrelated to capacity to give. It is related to generosity of spirit. Some have it. Some don't. Your first task once you've created a budget is to figure out who the givers are among those you know or can get to. Then you can develop a fund-raising strategy targeted at those people.

There are myriad political fund-raising tactics. They are the same ones you use at your church or women's group or Girl Scout troop. However, political fund-raising and charitable fund-raising are regulated differently. Consequently, you will need to learn and apply the rules for your locality. If you are in a federal race, you will have to learn and comply with those rules, too.

Whatever strategy you develop and whatever tactics you use, fund-raising is friend raising. People give to people they like, trust, and believe in. The best introduction in the world won't matter if you are not compelling.

Depending on the locale and size of a race, you may need professional fund-raising help. If you've participated in a training program, the trainers will be able to recommend fund-raising consultants. If not, your best bet is to talk to your local political party and colleagues who have already run races. They know who is good and available. Your local political party organization may also offer fund-raising training. You may even be able to share a staffer once you've decided on someone.

Mainly, like heart surgery, big-time fund-raising is a specialist's trade. Don't try to do it yourself. And as to small-time fund-raising, apply what you already know: ask those who care to give till it hurts. My favorite guide to grassroots fund-raising is *Successful Fundraising: A Complete Handbook for Volunteers and Professionals*, by Joan Flanagan.

Because political fund-raising includes asking for major gifts, here is an article that will orient you to how to think about major gifts: www.tgci.com /magazine/Getting%20Major%20Gifts.pdf.

Political Action Committees

Political action committees (PACs) raise money to support candidates. Some offer training and education programs for prospective candidates. Joining a PAC and becoming a PAC donor also are a good ways to learn about politics and government, about what it's like to be a candidate, how to build a network of like-minded colleagues, and how to be an influential person in the political arena and become a leader.

Because PACs are significant contributors to political campaigns, more and more are being formed. Here is a link to a list of Republican and Democratic PACs focused on women candidates, CAWP Women's PACs and Donor Networks: www.cawp.rutgers.edu/education_training/resources _for_candidate_campaign/documents/pacs.pdf.

Learning the Issues That Will Matter

★ ★ ★

To develop your issue expertise, you will begin by learning about the issues that concern your community. However, as you assume office or run or seek appointment to regional or state or federal office, you will need to become an expert on your portfolio of issues.

Research on women candidates proves that women usually run because they care about issues. (See the work of CAWP and Jennifer Lawless.) The research also proves that women officials introduce legislation that benefits women, children, and families more frequently than men do. For both of these reasons, it's important that you become an expert on the issues that affect the health and welfare of your community, issues uniquely of concern to women and girls, and legislation or policies that already exist that you can propose for your constituency.

Below is a list of selected national organizations that compile legislative data, conduct research, publish reports, sponsor educational conferences, and/or advocate for legislation, programs and policies to improve the status of women, girls, and their families.

Alan Guttmacher Institute
125 Maiden Lane, 7th Floor
New York, NY 10038
(212) 248-1111; fax (212) 248-1951
www.guttmacher.org

American Association of University Women
1111 16th Street NW
Washington, DC 20036
(202) 785-7700; fax (202) 872-1425
www.aauw.org
E-mail: connect@aauw.org
(Also a membership organization with local chapters)

American Legislative and Issue Campaign Exchange (ALICE)
University of Wisconsin, Madison
7122 Social Science Building
1180 Observatory Drive
Madison, WI 53706
(608) 890-4879
alicelaw.org
E-mail: alice@alicelaw.org

The Brookings Institution
1775 Massachusetts Avenue NW
Washington, DC 20036
(202) 797-6000
www.brookings.edu
E-mail: communications@brookings.edu

Center for American Progress
1333 H Street NW, 10th Floor
Washington, DC 20005
(202) 682-1611; fax (202) 682-1867
www.americanprogress.org

Center for Women Policy Studies
1776 Massachusetts Avenue NW, Suite 450
Washington, DC 20036
(202) 872-1770; fax (202) 296-8962
www.centerwomenpolicy.org
E-mail: cwps@centerwomenpolicy.org

Children's Defense Fund
25 E Street NW
Washington, DC 20001
(800) CDF-1200
www.childrensdefense.org
E-mail: cdfinfo@childrensdefense.org

Girl Scouts of the USA
420 Fifth Avenue
New York, NY 10018-2798
(800) 478-7248
www.girlscouts.org
(Also a membership organization with local chapters)

Girls, Inc.
120 Wall Street
New York, NY 10005-3902
(212) 509-2000
www.girlsinc.org
E-mail: communications@girlsinc.org
(Also a membership organization with local chapters)

Institute for Women's Policy Research (IWPR)
1200 18th Street NW, Suite 301
Washington, DC 20036
(202) 785-5100
www.iwpr.org
E-mail: iwpr@iwpr.org

National Council for Research on Women
11 Hanover Square, 24th Floor
New York, NY 10005
(212) 785-7335
www.ncrw.org
E-mail: contact@ncrw.org

National Network to End Domestic Violence
1400 16th Street NW, Suite 330
Washington, DC 20036
(202) 543-5566; fax (202) 543-5626
www.nnedv.org

National Partnership for Women & Families
1875 Connecticut Avenue NW, Suite 650
Washington, DC 20009
(202) 986-2600; fax (202) 986-2539
www.nationalpartnership.org
E-mail: info@nationalpartnership.org

National Sexual Violence Resource Center
123 N. Enola Drive
Enola, PA 17025
(717) 909-0710; fax (717) 909-0714
www.nsvrc.org
E-mail: resources@nsvrc.org

National Women's Law Center
11 Dupont Circle NW, Suite 800
Washington, DC 20036
(202) 588-5180
www.nwlc.org
E-mail: info@nwlc.org

National Women's Studies Association
11 E. Mount Royal Avenue, Suite 100
Baltimore, MD 21202
(410) 528-0355; fax (410) 528-0357
www.nwsa.org
E-mail: nwsaoffice@nwsa.org

Roosevelt Institute
570 Lexington Avenue, 5th Floor
New York, NY 10022
(212) 444-9130
www.rooseveltinstitute.org

Wider Opportunities for Women
1001 Connecticut Avenue NW, Suite 930
Washington, DC 20036
(202) 464-1596
www.wowonline.org
E-mail: vstaples@wowonline.org

Women Employed
65 E. Wacker Place, Suite 1500
Chicago, IL 60601
(312) 782-3902; fax (312) 782-5249
www.womenemployed.org
E-mail: info@womenemployed.org

In addition, the National Coalition of Women's Organizations lists members by area of expertise and various kinds of reports and data at www.womens organizations.org.

Keeping up with the competition (which is mostly other women)

★ ★ ★

You need to be qualified for the position you seek, including being knowledgeable about the subject matter. For instance, if you're running for election to your local school board, you'll need to understand local tax policy as well as education policy. You will also need to know what's on the minds of the people whose vote you are seeking. Fifty-three percent of American registered voters are women. In most elections, more women than men vote. In my experience most local community leaders are women. Keeping up with these women who share your interests and concerns, and against whom you are competing, is imperative.

Women's Websites and Blogs

Here is a list of selected websites that include blogs on women's and family issues, interviews with women politicians, news reports on women's issues and politics, and/or reports on how the media covers women. This list includes major newsstand women's magazines and online magazines. Many have Facebook and Google pages, as well as Twitter feeds and Pinterest pages. Remember that you can join RSS feeds, news alerts, groups, and/or pages that match your issue and political interests in order to receive information daily or even more frequently.

Asian American Women on Leadership: www.aawolsisters.com
Better Homes and Gardens: www.bhg.com

Blogher: www.blogher.com (a website that contains thousands of individual blogs)

The Broad Side: www.the-broad-side.com

CafeMom: www.cafemom.com

CareerDiva: www.evetahmincioglu.com

Catalyst: www.catalyst.org

Cosmopolitan: www.cosmopolitan.com

Ebony: www.ebony.com

Elle: www.elle.com

Essence: www.essence.com

Family Circle: www.familycircle.com

Fem 2.0: www.fem2pt0.com

Feminist.com: www.feminist.com (with a variety of resources by topic area: www.feminist.com/resources/links/index.html)

Feministe: www.feministe.us

Feministing: www.feministing.com

Forbes Woman: www.forbes.com/forbeswoman

Glamour: www.glamour.com

Good Housekeeping: www.goodhousekeeping.com

Hello Ladies: helloladies.com

iVillage: www.ivillage.com

Jezebel: www.jezebel.com

The Juggle (*Wall Street Journal* blog): www.blogs.wsj.com/juggle

Ladies' Home Journal: www.lhj.com

Latina Expert: www.latinaexpert.com

MariaShriver/Architects of Change: www.mariashriver.com

Marie Claire: www.marieclaire.com

Momocrats: momocrats.com

Moms Rising: www.momsrising.org

More: www.more.com

Motherlode: www.parenting.blogs.nytimes.com

Ms. Magazine: www.msmagazine.com

Name It. Change It.: www.nameitchangeit.org

O, The Oprah Magazine: www.theoprahmag.com

Oprah: www.oprah.com

Pandagon: www.rawstory.com/rs/category/pandagon

Parenting: www.parenting.com

Real Simple: www.realsimple.com

Redbook: www.redbookmag.com

The Root: www.theroot.com

Seventeen: www.seventeen.com
She the People: www.washingtonpost.com/she-the-people
Vogue: www.vogue.com
Woman's Day: www.womansday.com
Women's eNews: womensenews.org
Women's Media Center: www.womensmediacenter.com
XX Factor (*Slate*): www.slate.com/blogs/xx_factor.html

Here is a link to *Forbes*'s "2012 100 Best Websites for Women": www.forbes
.com/sites/forbeswomanfiles/2012/06/20/top-100-websites-for-women-2012.

And here is the link to *Forbes*'s "The 10 Best Websites for Millennial Women": www.forbes.com/sites/meghancasserly/2012/06/20/the-10-best-websites
-for-millennial-women-2012.

Knowing What the Pundits Know, Sharing Your Views with Them, and Becoming a Pundit Yourself

★ ★ ★

You can't be influential or a leader or a winning candidate if you don't know what those who study and write and comment about politics in the general press have to say. They set the political stage as much as candidates do. You will also learn from them, at least the good ones. In the past, most people read a local newspaper to learn the news and experts' perspectives on it. These days, most of us go to the web and social media for these purposes.

Twitter, here you come, if you aren't there already. Facebook and Google are good, too, but most political pros constantly post to Twitter and frequently engage with one another, which is also quite instructive.

When you join Twitter, keep up with it; it's all about the exchange of the moment. Offer your own views on what these folks are saying; read the articles they post and share them with your followers on other social media. You'll quickly become a source yourself, which friends and future supporters will appreciate and which will position you as even more of a winner than you already are.

Writers and Commentators

Here is a list of the political writers and commentators I like because I learn a lot from them. I follow them on Twitter, TV, radio, and Facebook. And I faithfully read what they write. By all means, develop your own list, focusing on the issues and people most relevant to your interests and political plans.

Mike Allen, *Politico*: www.politico.com/reporters/MikeAllen.html

Jessica Arons: www.americanprogress.org/experts/AronsJessica.html

Matt Bai, *New York Times*: www.mattbai.com

Krystal Ball: www.krystalonline.com

Joanne Bamberger, *Pundit Mom*: www.punditmom.com

Emily Bazelon: www.slate.com/authors.emily_bazelon.html

Lisa Belkin: parenting.blogs.nytimes.com/author/lisa-belkin and www .huffingtonpost.com/lisa-belkin

Donna Brazile: www.donnabrazile.com

Irin Carmon, *Salon*: www.salon.com/writer/irin_carmon

Meghan Casserly, *Forbes*: blogs.forbes.com/meghancasserly

Chris Cillizza, The Fix (*Washington Post*): www.washingtonpost.com/blogs /the-fix

Gail Collins, *New York Times*: topics.nytimes.com/top/opinion/editorials andoped/oped/columnists/gailcollins/index.html

Bryce Covert, *Forbes*: blogs.forbes.com/brycecovert

Candy Crowley: sotu.blogs.cnn.com

S. E. Cupp: www.redsecupp.com

Maureen Dowd, *New York Times*: topics.nytimes.com/top/opinion/editorials andoped/oped/columnists/maureendowd/index.html

Gloria Feldt: www.gloriafeldt.com

Jacklyn Friedman: www.jaclynfriedman.com

Jennifer Granholm: www.jennifergranholm.com

Maggie Haberman, *Politico*: www.politico.com/reporters/MaggieHaberman .html

Melissa Harris-Perry: www.melissaharrisperry.com

John Harris, *Politico*: www.politico.com/reporters/JohnHarris.html

Chris Hedges, *Truthdig*: www.truthdig.com/chris_hedges

Samantha Henig, *New York Times Magazine*: 6thfloor.blogs.nytimes.com /author/samantha-henig

Melinda Henneberger, *Washington Post*: www.washingtonpost.com/blogs /she-the-people

Amanda Hess: www.slate.com/authors.amanda–hess.html

Linda Hirshman, *Slate*: www.slate.com/authors.linda_hirshman.html

Ilyse Hogue, *The Nation*: www.thenation.com/authors/ilyse-hogue

Arianna Huffington: www.huffingtonpost.com/arianna-huffington/

Sasha Issenberg, *Slate*: www.slate.com/authors.sasha_issenberg.html

Jodi Jacobson, *RH Reality Check*: www.rhrealitycheck.org/user/jodi-jacobson

Rita Jensen, *Women's e-News*: womensenews.org/meet-womens-enews-staff

Jodi Kantor, *New York Times*: www.jodikantor.net

Richard Kim, *The Nation*: www.thenation.com/authors/richard-kim

Ezra Klein, *Washington Post* Wonkblog: www.washingtonpost.com/blogs
/wonkblog/

Sarah Kliff, *Washington Post*: www.washingtonpost.com/sarah-kliff/2011/07
/28/gIQAoLzSfI_page.html

Alex Kotlowitz: www.alexkotlowitz.com

Rachel Maddow: www.rachelmaddow.com and maddowblog.msnbc.msn
.com

Amanda Marcotte, *RH Reality Check*: www.rhrealitycheck.org/blog/amanda
-marcotte and www.slate.com/authors.amanda_marcotte.html

Ruth Marcus, *Washington Post*: www.washingtonpost.com/ruth-marcus/2011
/02/24/ABjkDzI_page.html

Roland S. Martin: www.rolandsmartin.com

Robin Marty, *RH Reality Check*: www.rhrealitycheck.org/blog/3618

Mary Matalin: www.matalin.info

Clarence Page, *Chicago Tribune*: www.chicagotribune.com/news/opinion
/page

Susan Page, *USA Today*: usatoday30.usatoday.com/educate/college/careers
/profile10.htm

Kathleen Parker, *Washington Post*: www.washingtonpost.com/kathleen
-parker/2011/02/24/ABsg1XN_page.html

Katha Pollitt, *The Nation*: www.thenation.com/authors/katha-pollitt

Maria Shriver: www.mariashriver.com/

Nate Silver, *New York Times*: fivethirtyeight.blogs.nytimes.com/author
/nate-silver

Ben Smith, *Politico*: www.politico.com/blogs/ben-smith/

Elissa Strauss, *The Forward*: www.elissastrauss.com

Lynn Sweet: *Chicago Sun-Times*: blogs.suntimes.com/sweet/ and *The Hill*:
www.thehill.com/blogs/pundits-blog/277

Amanda Terkel, *Huffington Post*: www.huffingtonpost.com/amanda-terkel

Rebecca Traister: www.salon.com/writer/rebecca_traister/

Karen Tumulty, *Washington Post*: www.washingtonpost.com/karen-tumulty
/2011/07/15/gIQAMhWJGI_page.html

Jessica Valenti: www.jessicavalenti.com

Alex Wagner: tv.msnbc.com/shows/now-with-alex-wagner/

Joan Walsh, *Salon*: www.salon.com/writer/joan_walsh

Top Political News and Commentary Websites

Here is a list of the top political news and commentary sites, in order of size of readership.

HuffingtonPost: www.huffingtonpost.com
Drudge Report: www.drudgereport.com
Politico: www.politico.com
Salon: www.salon.com
Newsmax: www.newsmax.com
The Blaze: www.theblaze.com
CSMonitor: www.csmonitor.com
InfoWars: www.infowars.com
Washington Times: www.washingtontimes.com
RealClearPolitics: www.realclearpolitics.com
The Hill: www.thehill.com
DailyKos: www.dailykos.com
FreeRepublic: www.freerepublic.com
TalkingPointsMemo: www.talkingpointsmemo.com

Here is a link to Chris Cillizza's list of the best state political blogs: www .washingtonpost.com/blogs/the-fix/post/the-fixs-best-state-based-political -blogs-extended-edition/2011/08/03/gIQAZva4rI_blog.html.

Other Websites or Magazines That Frequently Write about Women in Politics and Women's Issues

Some are included in the previous lists. Here are some others:

The Atlantic: www.theatlantic.com
Daily Beast: www.thedailybeast.com
Newsweek: www.newsweek.com
Time: www.time.com
Vanity Fair: www.vanityfair.com

Becoming a Citizen of the World

★ ★ ★

Women all over the world are united in a campaign to advance women's opportunities, education, and political and public leadership. If you're interested in international issues or if international issues factor into your community life, you will want to pay attention. Here is a list of some organizations that do this work. As the web reminds us every day, we are all just a click away from one another.

CARE USA
151 Ellis Street NE
Atlanta, GA 30303
(404) 681-2552
www.care.org

The Girl Effect/International Day of the Girl
www.girleffect.org
E-mail: info@girleffect.org

Global Fund for Women
222 Sutter Street, Suite 500
San Francisco, CA 94108
(415) 248-4800; fax (415) 248-4801
www.globalfundforwomen.org

International Center for Research on Women
1120 20th Street NW, Suite 500 North
Washington, DC 20036
(202) 797-0007; fax (202) 797-0020
www.icrw.org
E-mail: info@icrw.org

International Women's Health Coalition
333 7th Avenue, 6th Floor
New York, NY 10001
(212) 979-8500; fax (212) 979-9009
www.iwhc.org
E-mail: info@iwhc.org

UN Women
405 East 42nd Street
New York, NY 10017
(646) 781-4400; fax (646) 781-4444
www.unwomen.org/

Vital Voices Global Partnership
1625 Massachusetts Avenue NW
Washington, DC 20036
(202) 861-2625
www.vitalvoices.org
E-mail: info@vitalvoices.org

Books about Seeking Political Office, Women's Leadership, and Women in Politics

★ ★ ★

Becoming a Candidate: Political Ambition and the Decision to Run for Office by Jennifer L. Lawless

Big Girls Don't Cry: The Election That Changed Everything for American Women by Rebecca Traister

Campaign Boot Camp 2.0: Basic Training for Candidates, Staffers, Volunteers, and Nonprofits by Christine Pelosi

Empowering Women for Stronger Political Parties: A Good Practices Guide to Promote Women's Political Participation by Julie Ballington

Full Frontal Feminism: A Young Woman's Guide to Why Feminism Matters by Jessica Valenti

Get Opinionated: A Progressive's Guide to Finding Your Voice (and Taking a Little Action) by Amanda Marcotte

The Girl's Guide to Being a Boss (Without Being a Bitch): Valuable Lessons, Smart Suggestions, and True Stories for Succeeding as the Chick-in-Charge by Caitlin Friedman

Going Rogue: An American Life by Sarah Palin

The Gospel According to the Fix: An Insider's Guide to the Less Than Holy World of Politics by Chris Cillizza

How Remarkable Women Lead: The Breakthrough Model for Work and Life by Joanna Barsh, Susie Cranston, and Geoffrey Lewis

How to Win an Election: An Ancient Guide for Modern Politicians by Quintus
    Tullius Cicero, translated and with an introduction by Philip Freeman
If They Only Listened to Us: What Women Voters Want Politicians to Hear by
    Melinda Henneberger
Leading From the Front: No-Excuse Leadership Tactics for Women by Courtney
    Lynch and Angie Morgan
Letitia Baldrige's New Manners for New Times: A Complete Guide to Etiquette by
    Letitia Baldrige
*Notes from the Cracked Ceiling: Hillary Clinton, Sarah Palin, and What It Will Take
    for a Woman to Win* by Anne E. Kornblut
Organize to Win: A Grassroots Activist's Handbook by Jim Brittell (www.britell
    .com/text/OrganizeToWin.pdf)
*PunditMom's Mothers of Intention: How Women & Social Media Are Revolution-
    izing Politics in America* by Joanne C. Bamberger
*Sisterhood Is Powerful: An Anthology of Writings from the Women's Liberation
    Movement* edited by Robin Morgan
Twenty Years at Hull-House by Jane Addams
Unbought and Unbossed by Shirley Chisholm
The Victory Lab: The Secret Science of Winning Campaigns by Sasha Issenberg
*What Women Really Want: How American Women Are Quietly Erasing Political,
    Racial, Class, and Religious Lines to Change the Way We Live* by Kellyanne
    Conway, Celinda Lake, and Catherine Whitney
Women and Politics: The Pursuit of Equality by Lynne E. Ford
Women in Politics: Outsiders or Insiders?: A Collection of Readings by Lois Duke
    Whitaker
*The Women's Media Center Media Guide to Gender Neutral Coverage of Women
    Candidates and Politicians* by Rachel Joy Larris and Rosalie Maggio
Why Women Should Rule the World by Dee Dee Myers

Movies and YouTube

★ ★ ★

There are lots of instructive movies about politics. Chris Cillizza has a great
    list in his book, *The Gospel According to the Fix.*
Bulworth, starring Warren Beatty and Halle Berry
Charlie Wilson's War, starring Julia Roberts and Tom Hanks
Election, starring Reese Witherspoon

Legally Blonde, starring Reese Witherspoon
Primary Colors, starring John Travolta
Wag the Dog, starring Robert De Niro and Dustin Hoffman

Speeches are frequently posted on YouTube. Recently, when I wanted to get a better sense of a politician I was going to meet, I went to YouTube and watched a couple of speeches and a press conference she gave. You can do the same—both to learn about others and for yourself.

Acknowledgments

★ ★ ★

As a child, I realized I might become a voice for women because of the example set by my parents, Mary Robinson Sive and David Sive, who were devoted to public service. Thank you, Mom and Dad.

I was inspired to write *Every Day Is Election Day* by the lessons of my personal heroines. When I've been down, and when I've been up, their unceasing assertion of their birthright to public power in service of the public good has kept me going.

These women are: Shirley Chisholm, member of Congress and first African American woman candidate for president, whose autobiography says it all: *Unbought and Unbossed*; Jane Addams, the first woman to win the Nobel Peace Prize and the first Chicago community organizer; Ida B. Wells, crusading civil rights activist and journalist; Millie Jeffrey, Iowa farm girl, labor leader, and founder of the National Women's Political Caucus, who taught my generation how to be politically successful; Addie Wyatt, a Mississippi farm girl who coached presidents and kings and the rest of us how to stand up straight; Maria Cerda, daughter of Chicago and Puerto Rico; Bella Abzug, who gave me just the kind of hell I needed when I was starting out; and US senator Barbara Mikulski, the longest-serving woman in Congress, who I advanced once long ago on a cold winter day in Chicago.

Laurie Abkemeier is the literary agent of my dreams: smart, demanding, witty, wise, and thoughtful. Thank you, Laurie.

Lisa Reardon edits books about women for the same reason I write about women. She wants us to learn and to take heart from each other. Lisa: thank you for thinking my advice should be shared.

The women I interviewed for this book are thoughtful, generous, plucky, and committed to a better world. Thanks to all of you: the Honorable Deanna Archuleta, the Honorable Monica W. Banks, Frances Beinecke, the Honorable Carol Bellamy, the Honorable Molly Bordonaro, the Honorable Sharon Weston Broome, the Honorable Caroline Casagrande, the Honorable Barbara Flynn Currie, Rachel Durchslag, Ellen Chesler, the Honorable Betsy Gotbaum, Lori Healey, the Honorable Catherine D. Kimball, Shelby Knox, the Honorable Mary Landrieu, the Honorable Ludmyrna Lopez, the Honorable Lisa Madigan, Kimberly Merchant, the Honorable Aidan Myhre, the Honorable Gwendolyn Page, Lisa B. Percy, the Honorable Toni Preckwinkle, Cecile Richards, the Honorable Ilana Diamond Rovner, Bettylu Saltzman, the Honorable Jan Schakowsky, Mary Robinson Sive, Melody Spann-Cooper, the Honorable Debbie Stabenow, Julia Stasch, Laura Tucker, and the Honorable Melanne Verveer.

There are lessons here from the political lives of President Barack Obama and First Lady Michelle Obama, the Honorable William Jefferson Clinton and Secretary of State Hillary Rodham Clinton, First Ladies Eleanor Roosevelt and Nancy Reagan, Secretary of State Madeleine Albright, Secretary of State Condoleezza Rice, the Honorable Michele Bachmann, the Honorable Tammy Baldwin, Krystal Ball, the Honorable Catherine Bertini, the Honorable Barbara Byrd-Bennett, Norma Sanders Bourdeaux, the Honorable Carol Moseley Braun, Donna Brazile, Carol Burnett, the Honorable Cheri Bustos, the Honorable Shirley Chisholm, the Honorable Ertharin Cousin, Stephanie Cutter, the Honorable Tammy Duckworth, Sandra Fluke, Betty Friedan, the Honorable Tulsi Gabbard, the Honorable Kirsten Gillibrand, the Honorable Ruth Bader Ginsburg, the Honorable Nikki Haley, the Honorable Kamala Harris, Melissa Harris-Perry, the Honorable Maggie Hassan, the Honorable Heidi Heitkamp, Mary Kay Henry, Susan Hill, Jennifer Hing, the Honorable Mazie Hirono, Cheryle Robinson Jackson, the Honorable Bernette Johnson, the Honorable Shelia Johnson, the Honorable Emil Jones Jr., the Honorable Connie Marie Kelley, the Honorable Amy Klobuchar, Lisa Lee, the Honorable Earl Long, the Honorable Huey Long, the Honorable Mia Love, Mary Matalin, the Honorable Claire McCaskill, the Honorable Bridget Mary McCormack, Katherine McWatt, the Honorable Barbara Mikulski, Andrea Mitchell, the Honorable Susan Molinari, the Honorable Cecilia Muñoz, the Honorable Patty Murray, the Honorable Sarah Palin, the Honorable Nancy Pelosi, the Honorable Christine C. Quinn, the Honorable Dana Redd, the Honorable Ann Richards, the Honorable Cathy McMorris Rodgers, Desirée Rogers, the Honorable Debbie Wasserman Schultz, Cybill Shepherd, Maria Shriver, the Honorable Sonia Sotomayor, the Honorable Katharine St.

George, Mavis Staples, the Honorable Elizabeth Warren, and the Honorable Harold Washington.

Many thanks to all those who helped me bring this book to life, beginning with Anna Eleanor Roosevelt, my longtime friend and colleague, for writing the foreword. Thanks to Elizabeth Austin, Traci Baim, Martha Bergmark, Willa Bugnon, Ellen Cohen, Leslie Combs, Jean de St. Aubin, Bob Deans, Kim DeLatte, Carol Dinkins, Erin Donar, Tiffany Dufu, Judy Gaynor, Ingrid Goncalves, Peter Guralnick, Andrea Hagelgans, Sara Hays, Henry Henderson, Linda Hirshman, Mary Hughes, Derrick Johnson, Beverly Jones Heydinger, Scott Kastrup, Valerie Keitt, Victor and Sarah Kovner, the Keeler Keg, Blair Kilpatrick, the Honorable Clyde W. Kimball, Lydia Lazar, Ann Lewis, Ruth Mandel, Margaret McCamant, Becca MacLaren, Gayden Metcalfe, John Mitchell, Steve Mlenak, the Honorable Cindy Moelis, Kenyatta Morris, Portia Morrison, the Honorable Robert Morrison, Gina Natale, Jo Ann Nathan, Rich Nelson, Jessey Neves, Marissa Padilla, Jane Pinsky, Maura Possley, Alan Richmond, Annette Rodgers, Ellen Rodman, William "Brother" Rogers, Yumeka Rushing, Marcus Salazar, Jennifer Samawat, Bobby Silverman, Diane Skidmore, Steve Tabak, Brian Thomas, Debbie Walsh, Karen Wayland, Charles Weissinger, Cleo Wilson, and Leila Clark Wynn.

Index

★ ★ ★

About the Author

★ ★ ★

Rebecca Anne Sive writes and speaks on women's rights, American women's pursuit of political leadership and power, and the intersection of race and gender in American life and politics. Her writing for the *Huffington Post* and *RH Reality Check* has been regularly picked up by other national and international publications. She teaches on women and public leadership at the University of Chicago's Harris School of Public Policy Studies.

Rebecca is also a public affairs consultant who develops and leads programs to increase women's visibility and influence in American public life. Her unwavering goal is to advance women's economic security and reproductive autonomy so that American women may achieve their dreams of public leadership. She has been a public official, a board member, an officer of many public interest organizations, an adviser to other women leaders and to those seeking and holding public office, and an organizer of national women's issues agendas for presidents Carter, Clinton, and Obama.

In recognition of her leadership, Rebecca has received many awards, including distinguished achievement awards from her undergraduate alma mater, Carleton College, and the University of Illinois, from which she received an MA in American history. She lives in Chicago, which has been her home since her college years as a feminist activist. Rebecca may be found at www.rebeccasive.com.